Journeys of Hope II

12 more lives changed by God

Journeys of hope II

About the authors

Kathy Freeman

Kathy came to CAP in 2012 and is a brilliant writer. She has contributed to generating an average of 100 pieces of PR for the charity every month. She also researches and organises over 100 clients a year to represent CAP in the press, media and at events.

Daniel Furlong

Daniel joined CAP as part of our Reach intern programme in 2010, writing funding applications to charitable trusts. Daniel now leads this area and raises over £300,000 per year for CAP, in addition to helping our partner churches raise another £150,000 per year.

Ian Lynch

Ian joined the Communications team on Reach in 2012 and had a great year of contributing to the team, culminating in writing some brilliant chapters of this book. At the end of his year with CAP UK, Ian headed to CAP Australia on an International Reach placement, where he joined their Communications team.

Thanks also to our volunteer, Kate Martin, who wrote Sarah Jane's story.

Introduction

Josie Barlow

The Spirit of the Sovereign LORD is on me,
because the LORD has anointed me
to proclaim good news to the poor.
He has sent me to bind up the broken-hearted,
to proclaim freedom for the captives
and release from darkness for the prisoners,
to proclaim the year of the LORD's favour
and the day of vengeance of our God,
to comfort all who mourn,
and provide for those who grieve in Zion –
to bestow on them a crown of beauty
instead of ashes,
the oil of joy
instead of mourning,
and a garment of praise
instead of a spirit of despair.
They will be called oaks of righteousness,
a planting of the LORD
for the display of his splendour.

Isaiah 61:1-3

One thing that constantly amazes me is the way that God chooses to work through people. He chooses to show himself to the world not through big, impressive displays, but through people's changed lives. He said in Isaiah that they would be called 'oaks of righteousness, a planting of the Lord for the display of his splendour.'

This book is all about putting the beauty of God's transforming power on display. Only God can truly change a person's life; only God can give hope instead of despair; only God can bind up the brokenhearted and free those living in darkness.

When I meet our clients and hear their stories it is hard to truly imagine what it would be like to face what they faced; to live in such pain, deal with so much illness and experience shattered relationships. There is so much hidden suffering and poverty that surrounds us in our neighbourhoods. When faced with situations like these, we know that it doesn't have to be the end of the story. If God is allowed in, there can be a completely different future awaiting people. I hope these stories will inspire you about what God can do when we partner with him to give practical help and open the door for him to bring salvation and true healing.

The great news is that all of us can partner with God to change lives through CAP. Whether we pray, give, volunteer, work as a debt coach or at head office we are a team that God is using to change lives.

Matt and I joined the CAP team when John Kirkby showed up in our church in Cheltenham at the end of 1999. We had recently returned from the Dominican Republic where we had been working for a charity that provided primary education and health services in a poor village near the Haitian border. We had two of the best years of our lives, living with such amazing people who had such a joy for life despite having so little.

When we returned to the UK, God really used that time to cement in my heart and mind that I wanted to use my life to relieve poverty and see people come to know him. Shortly afterwards Matt went up to Bradford to meet John. When John heard about our heart and what we had been doing, he felt we were an answer to prayer. They had been asking God for two people to join CAP. One was to help oversee the new debt centre network, as the Aldershot CAP Debt Centre had just opened and four more debt centres were planned for January. John thought Matt would be great in this role. CAP was also looking for someone to concentrate on fundraising. As I had been doing fundraising in my job in Cheltenham, John offered us both jobs! After visiting John and his wife Lizzie, we knew this was an amazing opportunity. Within six weeks, we were living in Bradford and had joined the five staff working for CAP in two bedrooms in John's old house.

It has been such a privilege to be here from the beginning and to be part of the amazing adventure of Christians Against Poverty. We have had to press through so many obstacles and spend many years on our knees when we have been without the money to pay staff salaries, but we have always trusted our God. He is our guide and has always provided for us in the end!

We are passionate about empowering the church in every town and city in the UK to be the answer to the poverty and suffering they see in their neighborhoods through our CAP Debt Centres, CAP Money Courses and CAP Job Clubs.

I would like to give huge credit to the Communications Team at CAP. Particularly Kathy Freeman, Dan Furlong and Ian Lynch, who authored this book and wrote these amazing stories. Many hours were spent interviewing clients and bringing these stories to life from the hearts and minds of our clients. When I first read these stories, they brought tears to my eyes and gave me a massive determination to keep going to help even more people. I want to thank them for contributing so much to CAP by bringing the message of changed lives. Also, thanks to Claire Cowles who typeset the book and Viv Prior who designed the cover.

Matt and Josie Barlow

Matt and Josie were married in 1997 and have two children, Eve and Jed. Matt has been CAP's UK Chief Executive since 2006 and has won 'Best Leader' at the Sunday Times' 'Best Small Companies to Work For' four times. For nine years, Josie led fundraising at CAP, helping to increase income from £238k to £3.1m. In 2008, Josie was appointed as Communications Director to lead the teams who spread CAP's message and inspire people to give and get involved.

Dancing with Jesus

Sue Didi

'It's easy, Sue,' his gentle voice reassured me. 'All you have to do is hold my hands.' He stood before me, arms stretched wide, and I felt safe in his presence. 'Just take a step of faith,' his invitation continued, 'and come dance with me.'

With that, he faded away and I was left scanning the dark, hoping to catch another glimpse until a noise snatched my attention away. I registered the familiar sound and gradually opened my eyes to see the room around me coming to life with people worshipping loudly. As the song changed and new praises filled the air, I was amazed to hear the words that were now being sung: it was all about dancing with Jesus. 'Was it a coincidence?' I asked myself.

Shortly after the worship, someone got up to share their testimony. I was still trying to work out what the chances were of that particular song playing at that precise moment, when suddenly the person up front started speaking about dancing with Jesus! I nearly fell off my chair. For me it was the affirmation I needed that this wasn't a coincidence; this was God speaking to me. In that moment, I realised that I had been making the decision difficult. I knew I needed to let go and accept that it was easy, just like he said.

* * *

When Jan from Christians Against Poverty came to see me, I was in a really bad state of depression. Things had spiralled so far out of control that I had run up £40,000 of debt and had taken out loans that I couldn't pay back. I had no peace; by day I was harassed by calls from lenders and at night I was robbed of sleep by the worry that consumed my mind. It was endless.

I tried to ignore the incessant ringing of my phone and abandoned the unopened letters to a pile in the corner. I thought, 'What's the point? No one is listening. No one will help.' Too terrified to go out of the house in case someone appeared to push their way inside, I shut the door and hid. With each day that passed, I withdrew more and became a recluse. The pressure was extreme; I was desperate and suicidal.

It all started when I lost my job and house at the same time. For ten years, I worked for a teaching charity, but then we had a change of government and I was made redundant. I was renting a two-bedroom house on my own, so I phoned the letting agent and told them I was sure I would find another job soon. The very next morning, to my horror, they handed me an eviction notice.

My family lived far away. With no money and nowhere to go, I panicked as I pictured my life as a bag lady roaming the streets. After contacting the local council, I was relieved when they offered me a room in some sheltered accommodation. It was for people over the age of fifty-five, although most people there were well over seventy, but I was very grateful for somewhere to live. I had a roof over my head, but I had no money. I was told that there had to be an investigation into a property I owned previously with my ex-partner before I could receive any benefits. So I waited and waited.

Penniless and hungry, I borrowed from anyone I could, surviving on cheap bread and margarine. My mum did everything she could; she had savings that she gave to me, but she didn't have much and it soon ran out. I started to skip meals and couldn't pay for electricity. Desperate for money, I decided to take out a payday loan to keep me going. It was so easy; I just called them up and the money was in my bank within half an hour. I always thought I would be able to pay it back when the benefits arrived or I got another job. When neither happened, I panicked.

With the end of the month rapidly approaching, I took out a second loan to pay the first lender off. It brought a temporary relief, but as the investigation into my benefits dragged on I was forced to take out another loan to pay the last one. This cycle repeated and it wasn't long before I had taken out five loans. That's when the hounding began. It started with a few reminder texts, but soon I was besieged by calls. One particular creditor would ring five times a day despite the fact that I had already explained several times that I didn't even have money to feed myself. It was useless. Feeling alone and isolated, I withdrew into my tiny flat and spiralled further and further into depression.

For six painful months, the investigation continued. By this point, the Housing Association were concerned for me and they sent a Housing Officer who recommended I seek help. She told me about an organisation that had helped a previous tenant and suggested I give them a call. I was doubtful that anyone could help, but reluctantly took her advice and called CAP.

Straight away, Jan put me at ease. There was something about her that made me feel safe. She told me all about CAP and, as we talked about my debts, I felt like I could tell her anything. Handing over all my paperwork, she told me that CAP would contact all my creditors; I felt a huge weight lift off me for the first time in ages. No more phone calls! Soon after, Jan and people from the church turned up with shopping and filled my cupboards with food – it was amazing! A couple of times, a supermarket delivery would just turn up at the door. Soon the phone calls and threatening letters dwindled as three fantastic advisers at head office took care of my creditors. It felt like I could breathe again.

Jan was full of practical advice and gradually she encouraged me to leave the bubble I had created for myself in my room. Once a week I would go to the local drop in centre at Jan's church for free food parcels. The people there were very friendly and welcoming, but I was quick to retreat back to the safety of my hideaway. Gradually, Jan nudged me back out into the world; first for a coffee and then along to an Alpha course at church where I met other CAP clients who were in the same situation as me. It was a real comfort knowing that I wasn't alone in my debt. Another lady from church took me out and I slowly realised that it wasn't good for me to be inside with my own thoughts; dark thoughts that told me I was worthless.

As Alpha began to piece together some of the questions I had about God, I decided to go along to church and was taken aback by how lovely everyone was. Each week, I just couldn't believe that all these nice people were together in one place; two hundred people every Sunday. As I got to meet them, I was amazed at how every single one of them was so kind and loving. I had never come across anything like it before and I felt like I had a whole new family around me. I started to understand that church isn't about the building; it was about the people – even after two years, the people are still as lovely as when I first arrived.

When I first met Jan she asked about my belief in God. I told her that I believed in Jesus, but not in church. In the past, I had been to churches, but they were very religious and I didn't like all the rituals. I went to Sunday school as a kid and learnt about Jesus at school, but it was never in a way that affected my life. This was the first time I had been to a church that presented God in a relevant way. The way they preached the gospel was personal and real. It was all about Jesus and his life; how he died for us, and all the wonderful things he has given us.

I had been going to the Alpha course for a while but although it answered a lot of the questions I had, the idea of making a decision to follow God still felt too hard. I had a lot of things going on in my life that I felt were enough to deal with. The morning I saw Jesus, I was sat in church with my eyes closed, simply talking to God. I never expected him to actually appear to me, let alone ask me to dance with him! I couldn't quite believe that the Jesus I had heard about in stories could be so real. I had always avoided church and religion because it was all rituals to me, but then I saw the Lord himself reaching out his hands. I couldn't wait to tell Jan.

A month or two later, after choosing to make that step of faith to become a Christian, I got baptised and it was absolutely brilliant. Slowly, just as God changed me, I started to see other people change as they came to know Jesus. I would watch with intrigue as people took tentative steps towards God and then, when they found him, it was like they were suddenly glowing – I could just see the joy bursting out from within them. I decided to get more involved in church and helped set up a craft group to help people with confidence issues. Over time, God blessed the group and it was encouraging to see people come to know God and become part of the church family.

As I shared my story with people, I was surprised how it impacted others. People would come and ask me to pray for them. I guess I have been through a lot of things that others have, which allows me to talk openly and help others. As well as debt, I have been through violent marriages with partners who were alcoholics as well as having to overcome cancer and the loss of my child. When I look back to where I was, I can see that God has been with me all the way. He has totally healed me of depression. It wasn't instant, it took about three months, but that was quick considering that I had been on anti-depressants for seven years! The transformation in my life is huge and each day I feel better than the previous one.

With God, I have been able to do things I didn't think possible, like forgiving myself for the death of my child. Although it wasn't my fault, it was something that I hadn't been able to let go of for thirty-six years. She climbed out of the bedroom window and fell to her death when I was out at work and my sisters were babysitting. I had only had the job to get enough money for us to go on holiday and always felt that if I hadn't wanted the holiday so much, if I had only stayed at home, it wouldn't have happened. I knew the reality was that it could have happened even if I was there, but it is still too easy to think, 'If only, if only'.

When she died, I didn't think there could be a God who existed that could let that happen to my daughter and I denied him for many years after that. After Jan introduced me to church, I found a course with Resurrected Life Ministries. Whilst on the course, in one of the sessions we were told to visualise ourselves before we were born, in the arms of Jesus as a perfect person. I visualised my daughter instead of me. I hadn't meant to but that is just what came into my head. Just seeing how happy and cared for she was in the arms of Jesus enabled me to feel a huge weight lift. It was then that I felt a release of all the guilt I had held for thirty-six years.

After the session, I went to see my mother and we spoke about how I felt. She said she didn't know why I blamed myself because it wasn't my fault. One of my sisters was also there and she said that she had felt guilty all her life too. I didn't know she felt this way as none of us had ever talked about it. It was a great freedom for all of us to discuss things openly and realise there was no blame on anyone. I believe that was God's way of confirming what I had been through on the course. I still don't know why she died but I feel happy knowing she is with Jesus. She was like a little angel lent to me for a short time.

I have also seen miraculous things like people freed from addictions or healed of cancer – all sorts of wondrous things. For example, when I first saw one young chap he'd come into the church for food because he had no money. He looked like he was on death's door. He had been having epileptic fits every day and the stress of having no money was making him more ill. Since coming to know God, over the last year, he has really changed. He is stronger, looks healthier and his outlook on life is much more positive. He is more confident than he ever was and he now regularly comes to Bible study. There is also another lady who has overcome two episodes of cancer that involved huge operations, but she has come to know the Lord and is asking his help to kick her alcohol addiction. So far she has been successful. It's amazing. I see Jan and her husband like missionaries. They work for CAP to help people in debt and they also bring lots of people into church. Many, like me, are sceptical at first but then God changes their mind.

Earlier this year, I was overjoyed to receive the good news that I was finally debt free. I thought that would be the end of my journey with CAP, but God had other plans! Not long after, Jan told me that CAP was about to set up a new initiative called CAP Job Clubs that would help unemployed people find work again. With my previous experience as a teacher trainer, she thought I would be an ideal person to train as a Job Club Manager and open a CAP Job Club in our church. I was a little unsure, but I felt God nudging me and when I went along to the training I knew it was right.

I was really inspired after the training and was excited as I began to make preparations to launch the brand new CAP Job Club. One of the first things I did was arrange to see the local Jobcentre Plus Manager to discuss how we can work in partnership with them. Little did I know the appointment that God had set up for me.

I was just coming to the end of a great meeting with the lady who managed the Jobcentre Plus when I realised I had left a poster in my office that I should have brought with me. I offered to come back and drop it off another time, but instead she suggested coming to me. She told me she was keen to see our church as the building used to be a cinema and she was interested to see how it had changed. I was more than happy to show her around. When she arrived, the church was buzzing with activities such as the children's playgroup and deliveries for food parcels for those in need. The lady was quite astonished by all the things that went on and began to ask me lots of questions about God and the church. It was such a natural opportunity to share with her about Jesus and I was even able to offer her some prayer from the ministry team before she left!

It was encouraging to see how God was already using me in an unexpected way, but I still felt a little nervous about leading the CAP Job Club on my own. Whilst I had done lots of volunteering, I hadn't actually had paid work for three and a half years. I needn't have worried. When I began my introductory session with my first two delegates, it felt totally natural. First to arrive was a gentleman who had heard about the CAP Job Club through the church; he had been out of work for a year and a half and was keen to get some advice on CV writing.

The second was a lady who had only ever had one job in her life. She had heard about our CAP Job Club through the Jobcentre Plus and was overjoyed to discover it was at the church. It was an informal first meeting and both delegates left feeling very positive.

As I planned for my second week, I was blown away when I got an unexpected call to say that my first delegate had been offered a job! He had gone away and found work straight away. It was a welcome surprise and gave me a boost. I praised God for his provision and continued the next session with just the one other delegate. As she'd been out of work for a significant amount of time, it proved to be a great opportunity to provide her with much needed one-to-one support. I was looking forward to seeing her the following week when I got a call to say she wasn't coming back either. It turned out that she had been offered not one, but two jobs! I was over the moon; I never thought that I would see such quick results.

The journey I am on is only just beginning and it all started with a call to CAP. I just don't know what would have happened to me if Jan hadn't come around that day.

Released

Doris Brown

'**D**on't you dare leave me, John,' I sobbed miserably, 'don't you dare.' He'd complained about a tight chest the night before, but I hadn't thought anything of it. Now he was dead, and I was alone.

I used to watch people in debt on TV as they recounted lives of missed meals and sleepless nights. I'd shake my head at how they'd let themselves get into that situation; how they'd borrowed money, knowing they couldn't pay it back, or hadn't looked after their finances properly. 'How stupid can you be?' I'd mock, wondering how anybody could get into such a desperate state. 'That'll never happen to me,' I'd conclude confidently.

When John died, everything changed. The income was halved with the loss of his pension, and worse; I discovered a backlog of rent arrears and missed payments. We'd taken out the odd loan here and there for big purchases and a holiday to Australia, but I hadn't thought anything of it. The payments were so small – just ten or fifteen pounds – that I thought we were easily on top of them. With John's death, the combination of a huge reduction in income and a hidden debt situation turned small financial obstacles into huge money mountains that I simply couldn't get over.

I was surprised at the anger that welled up inside; why did John get a free pass from all the mess I was in? Together, we could convince ourselves that everything was fine, sweep it under the carpet and pretend it wasn't happening. I thought that, with John's death, the debt would be cleared, but all the bills and finances were in my name as I was always better with money. As far as anybody else was concerned, the sole responsibility for paying up was my own. I was terrified at the sudden isolation, and the fear twisted and distorted my emotions. I was looking for someone to blame at a time when I should have felt grief.

'I hate my husband!' I'd say without remorse. Bitterness grew like a gnawing parasite in my stomach and I spun into a cycle of feeling sorry for myself and angry with everyone else.

I had been abandoned in an unsolvable situation. I had my son with me and, while he did everything he could, I was in a mess. The rest of my family was over in Australia. The phone started ringing to ask for payments. At first the calls were friendly, just queries and reminders. I explained my situation to a sympathetic ear and was promised that the calls would stop. When it became clear that I had no money, the friendly calls turned to threats. The kind conversation from before was forgotten and the phone started to ring constantly. 'I have no money!' I'd plead, but the strangers on the end of the line would just shout louder and louder, demanding more and more.

I was bombarded on all sides and the pressure escalated. I had always been a fixer; if anything went wrong in the family I would have sorted it out, but this time I felt helpless. I looked for a way out, but my pride wouldn't let me apply for bankruptcy. People would find out and I couldn't face the shame. I thought back to the people on TV and suddenly saw my face instead of theirs. I was humiliated and vowed that nobody would ever know.

In my life's charade, I played the part of a woman that had everything together. I'd go out with my friends from the lady's club, wearing nice clothes and decorated in fancy makeup and beautiful hair. We'd go for day trips to the theatre or to visit an old castle grounds. We'd while away the afternoon amongst the gardens before sitting idly in a café, sipping tea and nibbling cake. I played my part well, talking light heartedly about daily life and future plans to mask the truth. Behind the scenes, when the curtain fell and I was alone again, the reality would return and I slipped slowly into despair. I was very good at bluffing my way through, avoiding having to pay for things with marvellous excuses. Sometimes I wonder if they knew all along. I went into denial, refusing to believe that the perfect life I'd planned had shattered.

I was balanced on a knife-edge of emotion. One stray thought or worry could tip me over, and I'd plummet into uncontrollable worry, bursting into tears at the slightest thing. Every morning would greet me with fear that would swell and grow as the day went on. From the moment I woke up, my thoughts were dominated by debt as the phone calls would begin, as if on cue. The worry was like a splinter in my mind, always there, twisting and churning to remind me that I had no hope. I looked for any way out, and my thoughts entertained the idea of ending it all. It was cold and the snow was falling. I could walk to the hills and sit there, waiting for hypothermia to take me away into an endless sleep. 'It would be easier than living with this,' I thought.

Just when I thought I had nothing left to cling to, the youth minister of the local church threw me a lifeline. We were on the same committee for a youth agency when we got talking. I was all over the place and upset so it all just came tumbling out. I told him about the mess I was in and he asked me if I had heard of a charity, Christians Against Poverty. He said they could help me. I was cautious, wondering what the catch was. I weighed up the options, realising that no matter what happened, anything had to be better than what I was going through. 'It can't get any worse,' I said, dialling the number.

I spoke to Jill, the Centre Manager of the local CAP Debt Centre. It was nice to speak to somebody on the phone without them demanding that I give them something. She was calm and reassuring as she explained about a home visit and arranged to come and see me. I dared to hope that I could be helped. She asked me to find every bank statement, bill and piece of paperwork that had drifted through the letterbox over the months, and keep them all together.

Jill came to see me together with another lady called Sheena, a lovely lady who volunteered as a Befriender for CAP. We sat in my living room as Jill explained how CAP worked. She wasn't fazed by the mountain of mail that was stuffed in giant envelopes on the coffee table. She was bubbly and chatty, like a friend who had popped over for a cup of tea. I'd expected her to be shocked at how bad things were, or find myself defending an onslaught of criticism, but it never came. Instead, I was covered in compassion and reassurance. Her calming presence was infectious and I found it hard to keep up my wall of bitterness, knowing that all she wanted to do was help me.

Before they left, Sheena offered to pray and I agreed. The words didn't mean much at the time; I just thought it was part of the package. I never expected anything to come of her prayers as I listened to her ask God to give me strength and pull me into his arms. But it was nice to know that she cared enough to ask God to help me. Then they left, taking the envelopes and my worries with them.

With CAP on my side, I could break out of my despair. They gave me the support I needed to face the fear and fight it. If the phone rang, I had the confidence to answer. 'CAP are dealing with this now,' I'd say, and hang up. The calls soon stopped. Sheena would give me a call from time to time to make sure everything was okay. We'd meet up for coffee and chat about normal things. She'd make sure I had enough food and was generally there to be a friend. Life wasn't easy, but knowing there were people who genuinely wanted to help me get through it was an immeasurable comfort.

When Jill invited me to come along to church, I thought it was the least I could do to go with her. I didn't expect to be welcomed with such warmth and love as soon as I stepped across the threshold. I had never met these people, yet they embraced me with such kindness that I couldn't hold back the tears. I was overwhelmed by their genuine compassion; they knew nothing about me, but saw me as a real person.

I decided to go on an Alpha course to learn more about God and Jesus. I had so many questions to ask and didn't hold back from asking them. I was awkward and difficult; I argued points and delved into difficult topics, keen to find out as much as I could and get answers to the questions I had. Then, at Christmas, the church had a day away in Carlisle. While we were there we were asked to come forward for prayer if we felt moved by the spirit. I felt nothing, so I just sat there. 'What a load of mumbo jumbo,' I said to myself. I remember looking at the people who had got up, thinking 'how stupid', when all of a sudden I realised I was stood next to them! I was amazed. I wasn't quite sure what had happened, but there I was and so they prayed for me. Jill was crying, I was crying – I couldn't deny it, but I hadn't meant to go up.

Despite this, I still felt I needed a nudge from God, just something to let me know he was there. I had been talking to a friend who had asked God for a sign and, overnight, her garden had blossomed with roses. I thought 'how wonderful', and so I asked him for a sign too. It didn't have to be roses, but I wanted something unusual and different to let me know he really cared.

The next day, my son bought me a new kettle. To anybody else, this would have been nothing – a nice gesture, perhaps – but of all the things he'd ever got me, none were practical gifts like a kettle! It was such an unusual thing for him to do and it made me wonder, 'Is this my sign?'

I started thinking about the turn around in my life; the fear that had once dominated my thoughts had been conquered, the hope I had for the future was restored and I had people in my life that I could rely on. Everything had been transformed – my life was the very sign that I had been looking for. Despite everything, I didn't feel like I'd make a very good Christian. I said I wouldn't get baptised; I just wasn't ready.

That night, I fell asleep with the TV on. I awoke in the middle of the night when all was quiet and still. On the screen, a group of people were standing in a river, the light dancing off the ripples. One of the men was submerged for a moment before coming out of the water, shimmering in the sun. 'I must be dreaming,' I concluded as I realised what I was watching. The next day, I checked the Radio Times – it was a programme on Jesus' baptism. I couldn't deny that this was what God wanted me to do and, soon after, I was baptised.

CAP continued to support me through everything that life could throw at me. They never abandoned me when things were hard. Better still, I made great friendships to enjoy the good times with and help cope with the obstacles when they came. Slowly, the pain of worry started to fade from my stomach. It was a gradual thing, but I would occasionally catch myself laughing and would think back to where I had been and the sheer terror I had felt.

Out of nowhere, I received a call from Jill asking if I wanted to go on a CAP holiday. 'I have no money!' I reminded her, wondering how she thought I'd ever be able to afford it. 'You don't need any,' was the reply. The holiday was fantastic; we stayed in log cabins and were really looked after. I had never had a holiday like it, with different sessions to get involved with and activities to do. I had so much fun and felt like a child, free from the worries and stresses of life, just for a weekend.

I've been debt free for three years now, but will always remember how CAP stepped in to help me when I was at my lowest point. I was so scared and vulnerable, trying to protect myself by blaming everybody else for my problems. With the confidence I had in CAP, I could open my heart to the support of the Church and the love of Jesus to transform me from the inside out. I have a new lease of life and a new outlook for the future. For a while, I was dead inside; it is nice to be among the living again.

Choosing God's way

Rakesh Kajal

It was almost too easy to do. I wasn't a genius and it wasn't a highly planned operation with a crack team of criminal masterminds. Fifteen years ago, I could stroll into a bank and set up an account in a fake name, then cash cheques for fifty or one hundred pounds at a time. I'd jump through loopholes in the Post Office system to get cash and then disappear again before anyone could notice. Sometimes, I'd con insurance firms with fraudulent claims. I moved from place to place and stripped my identity so that nobody could trace me. I hardly existed at all.

* * *

The heavy knocking threatened to break the door from its hinges, lock and all. I knew that there'd be no escape this time and almost welcomed the end of the chase. Years before, I'd have risked a perilous scramble through the window and down the fire escape, despite the steady staccato of rain that leaked from clouds above the Sheffield skyline. But I was tired of running; always looking over my shoulder as I moved from place to place in isolation, calling nowhere home and owning nothing.

'It's easy,' they'd said one afternoon as I was walking home from university, 'they'll never catch us.'

It had started small. Every now and again, urged on by the wrong crowd, we tried to outdo each other with bigger risks and larger cons. We lived the high life of small-time criminals for a while. Free money at that age went on anything we wanted it to, but it could never last. I soon found myself dropping out of university, subscribing to this dark new life and disowning who I was. I went on the run, changing my name countless times so that I could never be traced.

I always hated it, even in the very beginning. I had been brought up to be a good Hindu lad and I knew it was wrong, but I bowed to peer pressure. Existing in isolation and knowing that I was breaking the law was a constant tap on the shoulder, like a nagging reminder of all the wrong I was doing. I became increasingly frustrated and dissatisfied but it was everything I had become and, as a result, the only way I could live. I wasn't even careful; sometimes I'd use my own name and just move location. I should have known that it would catch up with me.

I stood in the magistrate's court, with the evidence brought before me like a slideshow of dubious memories. My past activities seemed worse when scrutinised by somebody who held my future in their hands. The consequences weighed down on me for the first time; I'd never really thought about what would happen if I got caught. Now, with the reality of an inescapable sentence before me, I was scared. I knew I didn't want to go to prison. I knew this wasn't the life that I wanted to lead. I waited in trepidation for the sentence to be read out.

'Conditional discharge.' I was stunned. I had been preparing for prison. Expecting to spend months of my life in further isolation, with no hope and no future. The end of the line. Perhaps the magistrate saw something in me, or maybe he could tell that I knew there was a better way to live.

'If I ever see you in this courtroom again,' he warned, 'there will be no leniency to your sentence. I will make sure that I personally deal with you. This is your one and only chance.'

I took it.

* * *

The conditions of my sentence required me to get a job immediately and report to the police once a month. I still couldn't believe that I had a chance to turn things around and gladly took the opportunity to do some honest work. Standing in the courtroom had shaken my confidence badly and I was determined to prove myself.

I got a job as a lab assistant; cleaning petri dishes, sterilising equipment and aiding with menial tasks. I was a glorified pot-washer, for all intents and purposes. The pay was very low, but it was a million miles away from my past life. A girl there was appointed as my mentor for the first few months and she quickly told me that she was a Christian. 'That's all I need,' I thought to myself, 'some do-gooder preaching morals at me'. However, she shared her faith in passionate and lengthy descriptions of a personal saviour and loving relationship with God. Every day, she'd chat about him and how I should come with her to church. I had no interest at first, but she was relentless and she had something about her that appealed to me. Finally, after three months, I agreed – if only to stop her from asking.

I had expected something different. I'd never been to church before, but always envisioned a quiet place. I imagined a small, cold room with long rows of hard wooden pews and robed choirs singing softly in melancholic Latin. I thought I'd be able to slip in and out without being noticed. Instead, I was greeted by warm handshakes and smiles and was invited to sit with a group of people. They welcomed a complete stranger into their church as though I was close family. I wondered if they'd be so keen to know me if they knew of the past I brought with me, yet something told me that they wouldn't have cared.

I felt unclean as I sat there, listening to the preacher share more about a man named Jesus. But then I looked up; behind the preacher was a giant banner. Two hands were chained together and I could relate to that. I felt just as chained by the activities I used to do. As I looked more closely, I realised the chain had been broken in two, and at the centre was the cross. I was struck by the message, 'Jesus breaks your chains'. I knew the image was meant for me and, in an instant, the cage of a disgraceful past shattered all around me and I broke down. In a heartbeat, I was transformed and knew Jesus was real.

My first steps of faith were difficult yet exciting. On the one hand, I was part of a community of caring people who helped nurture my relationship with Jesus. On the other hand, I struggled to change everything about my life. I felt convicted to be a better person – to be legal – but I lived with drug addicts, sleeping on the floor, and still went by a variety of aliases. The church helped me find a new place to live, all in my own name, and I had the opportunity to start again and to live properly for the first time.

Despite the clean slate, I couldn't escape the past. With everything in my own name now and registered to one address, creditors started crawling out of the woodwork and began a relentless campaign of reclamation. The letters started slowly at first, but soon became mountains of threats. Torrents of paperwork poured through the letterbox to carpet the floor and the phone would incessantly yell in shrill tones from the hallway. I knew it would just be another voice demanding money that I simply didn't have. My job barely paid enough for me to live, let alone pay back what they were asking for. I was in £37,000 of debt and running out of options.

I couldn't bring myself to tell anyone in church and put on a smiling mask instead to hide the shame I felt inside. I'd leave the house through the back door, just in case bailiffs were waiting on the other side. After work, I'd come home late so that I wouldn't be in when they hammered on the door, shouting demands through the letterbox. I spiralled into depression and my new faith was tested. Before, I could have run away from it, changed my name and pretended it wasn't happening. Now I had nowhere to turn and nobody to help. I was desperate.

One morning, in the middle of my lonely depression, God stepped in. Amongst the crisp white envelopes that landed on the doormat was a copy of 'Joy', a Christian magazine. Someone from church must have put it through my letterbox. Within its glossy pages, a tiny advertisement caught my eye, despite it being so small. It was for a debt counselling charity, Christians Against Poverty. Out of desperation, I made the call.

I was immediately put at ease by the calm voice at the other end. It was the early days of CAP, and the debt centre network didn't cover my area. I thought my lifeline had been cut short before I'd even had the chance to grab it. My despair was turned to joy when I was told that Carlo, a Centre Manager from the Nottingham CAP Debt Centre, would make the lengthy drive up to Sheffield to see me.

When he stepped through the door, I was stunned by the calm that swept in with him. He greeted me as a person, not like the failure I felt. To him, I wasn't another poverty stricken statistic that needed rescuing from a mire of issues I'd brought on myself. He could see the reality of my desperate situation and wanted to give me the support to get myself out of it. Before we even talked about my debts, he prayed for me. I felt so at ease knowing that he was bringing God into the situation.

'Don't hold back about your debts,' he said, 'I need to know everything.' For the first time, I revealed the full extent of it all. I hadn't told anyone before and it was a relief to finally let it out. A weight lifted from my shoulders with each revelation. Carlo didn't judge me; he just recorded everything and collected the piles of paperwork. I'd expected some sort of verbal slap on the wrist or lecture about my mistakes, but it never came.

When he left, I was so reassured. He was such a genuinely nice guy who had taken the time to travel up to see me. When he told me that everything was going to be sorted out, I believed him. I knew that I had the support I needed to begin piecing my life back together.

I'd like to say that from then on it was easy, but it wasn't. I'd opted to go down a repayment route and pay off my debts without bankruptcy. It would take at least five years to pay off, but I was up for the struggle. I was left with a very tight budget and hardly any money, but I had started to chip away at the debt. It felt good to break the cycle of being on the run and always worrying about creditors and bailiffs. After CAP had negotiated repayments with them, they stopped calling and sending letters. I could see the light at the end of the tunnel and, for once, it felt like I could reach it.

Over time, things started to slot together elsewhere in my life like a jigsaw. I was invited by my pastor to go on a mission trip to India. God miraculously provided for all my expenses and I continued to see his favour in my life. The airline even made a mistake with my ticket and had to upgrade me to Business Class! On the very last day of the trip, I met the woman who would become my wife. It was instantaneous; I knew straight away that we were meant to be together and I didn't delay. We borrowed a wedding dress and got married the very next day! My new wife, Anita, came to England a few months later to join me.

Finances were an increasing struggle now that we were a family. I looked for work, scouring websites and newspapers for any hint of a job. Ironically, I saw a job for the Inland Revenue and I'm not sure what made me apply in light of my financial troubles and criminal past. 'I won't get this in a million years,' I said as I posted off the application. Little did I know that God was paving the way for me.

I got the job as a tax assistant. Stunned by God's provision, I worked hard, taking as many opportunities as I could. The downward spiral of financial woe straightened out and became an escalator to a hopeful new start. Over the following year, I rose through the ranks and became a senior officer, and I was also nominated to become a magistrate in the very court I was convicted in. Opportunities continued to open up for me. I knew at that point that everything had come full circle and I had really turned my life around. I had always thought that I could use my experiences to reach people in a similar situation to where I was. I wanted to share my story and let people know that there was a way out. I could stand there as a person who had been through it and confidently tell them that there was hope and this wasn't the end for them.

Out of the blue, the news came that I had paid off all my debts. I'd simply been following the budget that had been put together since day one, paying into my CAP Account when I needed to and slowly walking the path to becoming debt free. It was liberating to be finally free of it all. God has honoured me in taking that step of faith to trust CAP and repay all that I owed. I started to think about how I could give something back. I was already a Life Changer, making a monthly donation to the charity, but I felt God nudging me inside to do something more for him.

My wife and I joined a church and wanted to do something through the church; something that would give hope to the local community and enable me to reach out to people that were desperate for help. I'd sit in church and see shadows of people walking past the window who had no idea that there was a sanctuary of hope right on their doorstep.

I looked for a way to spread the message in this deprived area. Over a short period of time, God reminded me of how CAP had helped me and slowly the idea of opening a CAP Debt Centre began to germinate. It was such an obvious response that I almost missed it. I brought the idea to the leadership team, who said they'd been waiting a long time for someone to do something like this and would support me all the way. That was the confirmation that this is what God had in mind for me.

Now, I get the opportunity to reach out to those who were in the same place as I was. I step into the homes of vulnerable and marginalised people, and see the same look of desperation in their eyes as I saw in my own, years before. I can bring with me a message of hope and tell them that there is a way out of their situation. It's an amazing privilege and I absolutely love it!

My journey has been a long and difficult one, but looking back, I can see God has always been with me. Though the path wasn't always easy to walk on, I have been blessed by staying on course. Due to a serious illness, my wife and I were told we could never have a baby, but I am now the proud father of a beautiful seven-year-old daughter. She is known as 'the miracle baby' in church and shows me that God is above all things and works all situations for good. Looking back, I can see so many examples of how he has worked goodness into every part of my life.

What I have learned in my life so far is that God loves people hugely and that people matter to him, even when they think he doesn't matter to them. Thankfully, he sees our lives as more than a collection of mistakes and is ready to give life, and life to the very full.

Escaping the past

Wendy Preston

From the age of nine, I can't remember a time in my childhood where I wouldn't be sitting alone, sobbing into my knees so nobody could hear me as I shuddered in the darkness. I'd stay there until there were no tears left to cry and exhaustion would take over. These days, I hear people talk about their childhood with smiles as they remember family holidays to the seaside and eating sticky ice creams on hot summer days. I can't relate; I will never understand why four men snatched my childhood from me, not seeing the fear in my eyes, or hearing my cries of pain as they loomed over my fragile frame and took my innocence. I didn't understand. I was only nine years old.

* * *

The morning announces itself with a fanfare of birdsong and the sun leaking through a tiny gap in the curtains. I've never noticed it; each day before this was just a struggle to the next, and mornings were just the start of more pain. I've been awake for hours, the excitement of leaving it all behind keeping me from sleep as I entertained the idea. My bag is packed with the few things I own and I smile, surprised that I still know how to; it's been such a long time.

Today, I'm moving in with a man who loves me. I don't know many men, so when this one tells me he is going to take me away from the hurt, I don't hesitate to buy into his promises. The crumbling relationship with my dad has all but eroded away, and I want nothing more than to escape it all, to wake up every day with the same hope for the future as I have this morning.

It lasts for a while, but then the anger starts. It's nothing at first; just little arguments that all couples have. 'This is normal,' I tell myself, 'it's just part of the relationship.' But it only gets worse. The first time he hits me, I'm not surprised. In fact, I almost expect it; it's all I've ever known.

Tonight, I'm tossed around like a rag doll, but I don't feel it anymore. He pins me to the wall with such a force that it knocks a glass of water from the counter. That's my fault too and he tells me that I deserve the punishment that's coming. The full force of him rains down on old bruises, barely healed from the last beating. The room swims in flashing lights and he only stops when he sees our four-year-old child cowering in the doorway; her hands clamped over her ears and her eyes screwed shut. He stamps out of the kitchen without a word and moments later, a car door slams and an engine roars to life. I slide down the wall and hug my knees; the choking sobs finally coming. I pull my baby to me and we cry together, clinging on to all we have left. I try to calm her, stroking the tear-drenched hair from her face. I see a familiar fear in her tiny eyes and I'm nine years old again. 'We're leaving,' I whisper.

For the second time I'm escaping, not knowing where I'm going, or how I'm going to get there. I hurry through the streets of Dublin, clutching a single bag in one hand, and my daughter in the other. Every growling car engine behind us makes my heart pound, thinking it might be him. I feel exposed and guilty, like a criminal on the run. Passers by stare at me accusingly, but I press on, deciding what to do. I have to get as far away as I can, away from him, where he will never find us. I head for the train station.

I look at the map, with the train lines sprawling across the face of Ireland like an uneven web. The choice is easy; Coleraine is the furthest place away, right at the end of the line. I buy a ticket, exchanging the last of my money for a glossy square of card - a ticket to a new life. As the train hisses to a stop at the platform and the doors slide open,

I take one fleeting glance back. Then I'm swept into the carriage with the crowds. I find a seat and stare out of the window as the scenery slides past. Snapshot memories of my life scroll by, getting more unfamiliar as the train races on. It plunges into a tunnel and everything is dark for a few moments. Then it bursts into the light and I don't recognise the view.

It takes the best part of ten years to feel any form of normality. Everyday tasks are huge challenges that I have to build myself up to. I can't stand going outside; a fear grips me as soon as the door is opened and swells until I feel ill. Venturing outside to pop to the local shop makes me physically sick, and so I rarely ever leave the house at all. I spend days at a time locked away in my bedroom. I feel safe there, where nobody can find me.

It takes therapists to help me confront the years of abuse. They sit me down and talk to me in soothing voices, gently taking me back through an album of painful memories. I relive the worst moments of my life in those sessions. Despite everything they try to do to help me put the past behind me, I come to realise I will never fully move on – I just have to accept what has happened. With their help, I learn to cope. I'm taught to take each day as it comes and find ways to ease the knot of fear in my stomach. My confidence grows as I settle into a routine that is close to normality. Eventually, I feel ready to get a job.

I'm thrilled to find work and finally feel like I'm moving on. The dark grasp of the past that once consumed me starts to lose its grip as I make plans for the future. Going to work feels fantastic. I feel normal, earning money to support my daughter and I. Leaving the house becomes easier and I feel strong and independent, knowing I can finally start living the life I've been waiting to live for so long. But then, just as before, when I tentatively put out my hands to climb out of the pit of despair, I'm thrown back in and all I've worked for tumbles down on top of me.

Somehow, my manager finds out about my troubled past and uses it to bully me, tugging on the single thread that's keeping everything together. The past ten years of progress begin to unravel and my life spirals out of control. The barriers I'd spent months building against the depression and guilt come crashing down. I try my best to beat it, holding it off for as long as I can, but the voice of the therapist gets quieter and quieter until it's lost in the turmoil. Depression builds over me like a storm and the fear swells again. Stepping outside brings back anxiety and illness, and every day gets harder to face. Within six months, I'm signed off work and back in my bedroom. I realise I am never going to escape.

As I wake up each day, the woman staring back at me in the mirror isn't living; she is simply waiting to die. The world doesn't want me and I've got nothing left to give. I've tried to pick myself up and get back on the horse, I've been knocked down too many times to try building myself up again. I decide that I'm just not meant to have a better life and that I deserve what I've got. I toss another dose of anti-depressants into my mouth, but they do little to lift me from despair. My daughter leaves me food on the stairs, the furthest I ever get from the covers of my bed.

I make the decision to put money towards the gas bill today, but that means I won't be eating. The debts have been mounting for a while and, without a job, I can't afford to feed us and pay the bills. Almost daily, the landlord demands rent with increasing threats, and an avalanche of payment reminders, final demands and court actions tumble through the letterbox with a flutter of noise that makes me wince. I scoop them into a bag, unopened, with the mountain of others that look exactly the same: 'FINAL

DEMAND', 'RESPOND NOW OR FURTHER ACTION WILL BE TAKEN' – red ink shouting up from beneath the plastic windows of each envelope. At first, I felt guilty and worried when the letters and phone calls came, but now the phone rings unanswered and the letters are ignored. It's become almost like a ritual and I don't even think about it anymore. I wonder how long I can hold them off. Each night, I fall asleep hoping it will be for the last time, and I can't stomach the disappointment when I wake up.

I'm thrown a lifeline when my neighbour tells me that a church is giving away free food. I've come to learn that nothing in life is free, and wonder what they want in return. The cupboards and fridge are empty and the idea of a decent meal breaks through my reservations – the empty growl in my stomach convinces me to go. I take a deep breath before stepping outside. The walk is long and each step throws up more doubts. More than once, I think about turning back, but one step follows the other. 'What have I got to lose?' I tell myself.

I step through the door, with my head down. 'Get the food parcel and get back to your bedroom where it's safe,' I tell myself, over and over. But then I look up. All around me are warm smiles and faces filled with love. It seems to radiate from them and I can't help but feel overwhelmed by their compassion. They invite me to sit and talk, and I'm washed with wave after wave of kindness. They bring me food, but don't rush me to leave and I find myself wanting to stay. For once, somebody just wants to make it better. Tears I've held back for years come streaming out. They don't judge me; they just listen with infinite patience as I talk about my situation. My past comes flooding out as I tell them of my despair. Each revelation makes me feel just a little better; sharing what I'm going through with somebody else makes it somehow easier to bear.

They tell me about a charity that can help with my debt situation – Christians Against Poverty. These people have such confidence that I can be helped that I take their advice. Something nudges me on; a quiet voice at the back of my mind that gives me the confidence I need to walk into their office and book an appointment – I just know it's the right thing to do. One last shot at turning things around. One last go at life.

When I meet Ian, the local CAP Debt Coach, he brings with him that same peace I'd felt in the church. I'm so nervous at first; I've never known a man who hasn't hurt me in the past and I can't help but think this man will join the others. It's all I've ever known. But then he starts talking to me, treating me with infinite care and respect and warmly explaining about whom CAP are and what they can do. I'm surprised when I find myself opening up and talking about my situation to him.

A brief chat turns into an afternoon of conversation. For over three hours, we talk about how CAP can help me to get out of debt. He asks me not to hold anything back, so I sheepishly produce eight years' worth of bills and letters, and reveal how far behind I am with the rent. With each revelation of my troubles, I expect him to frown, roll his eyes and say that it's just too hopeless for him to help. I expect to be made to feel small and stupid, like I always have been before. Instead, he simply collects it all together and reassures me it's going to be okay.

Every shameful debt I bring up is greeted with a compassionate smile as though he's seen it all before and I dare to hope that even I can be helped. He tells me that, together, we're going to turn things around. As I hand over the stress of my debt, I'm struck by a sense of confidence. I just know that it's going to turn out alright. I begin to believe that I do deserve better than an empty life; that there is more for me. The fear that had gripped me for so long begins to fall away as the hours pass. Peace fills the room and drives back the smog of despair. I feel like I did in the church, when a comforting arm held me as I poured out my troubles. 'What is this?' I ask myself; 'what do these Christians have that gives them such peace, and how can I have it too?'

My family was always very anti-Christian, but the God they had told me about was nothing like the personal saviour that Ian describes when I ask him about it. He tells me that the creator of the universe, who knows every hair on my head, loves me and cares about me so deeply that he gave up his only son so that I could call him Father. As Ian shares his faith with me, I understand why he is so calm; he knows that he is loved beyond recognition. He describes a relationship with Jesus that gives him joy and hope. It's all I've ever wanted and I decide there and then to give my life to God. In just a few short hours, my life has been turned upside down; the feeling of freedom is incredible. I know that my fear is gone when I give Ian a hug. I've not hugged a man since I was a child.

Putting my trust in God and CAP gives me the support I need to start the journey. It's difficult but I know that I am not alone; they will be with me for every step. We work out a budget that gives me clear direction on what I can spend. It's tight and takes some getting used to, but I know that CAP are fighting my corner, negotiating with creditors and looking after my finances. The letters and phone calls stop and I can pay my rent. It's releasing and gives me the courage to stop hiding in my room and, instead, step confidently into a world that is suddenly filled with a million opportunities.

* * *

I smile at the unopened bottle of anti-depressants on the bathroom counter. It's been so long since I've taken one, I'm not sure why I still have them.

I suppose it reminds me of how far I've come since working with CAP. It's been just seven months since Ian first stepped through my door, but it feels like a lifetime ago.

I took my faith and ran with it, eager to get involved with the local church and the people that embraced me so willingly before they even knew me. I start going to a small group to learn more about God. Every session reveals more about a father who loves me and has plans for me. When I'm asked whether I want to be baptised, I jump at the chance to declare that I've started a new life with God. I tell everyone I meet about how God has set me free.

My journey isn't over. I still have a long way to go before I'm debt free, but I know that by putting my trust in CAP and my faith in God, I will reach my goal with pride and with my head held high. I know I will have faced my debts and cleared them, instead of hiding from them and hoping they would just go away. Now, I embrace life instead of waiting to die. I dream of owning my own business now and with a business course on the way, my dream is just over the horizon. I have family and friends who love and accept me for who I am. The relationships with my father and ex-partner have both improved and I rejoice in God and life. My life isn't perfect, but it is filled with hope, joy and love.

Freedom

Brian Scott

Sometimes, us men can be our own worst enemy. I was brought up a true Scotsman and taught to be in charge of the family. If you get yourself in trouble, then you get yourself out. But I didn't feel in charge. Instead, I felt like a failure. We barely had enough to get through the month and things were getting worse. If something cropped up, like something needing to be replaced in the house, then that was it. I had a wife and two small boys to provide for and it was a constant struggle just to pay the bills. 'This isn't how it's meant to be', I would think to myself; 'I am the head of the household, I am meant to be the breadwinner'. I felt too embarrassed and ashamed to admit I couldn't cope. Now I know that it takes a huge amount of courage to ask for help, and I am so glad I did.

* * *

I had an accident at work, which left me with chronic pain. I had been working as a nurse in a cardiac catheter lab, taking photographs of patients with heart conditions. I managed to dislodge a vertebra in my back and had to take time off work. When I returned, I soon realised it was a mistake. Due to the equipment we were using, we needed to wear lead jackets to protect ourselves. Each jacket, weighing thirty to forty pounds, was very heavy, and we wore them for around four hours at a time. The prolonged compression on my spine led to nerve damage. It left me in constant pain and I started to lose feeling in my left leg. I was medically discharged from work and told that I may be in a wheelchair for anything from two to twenty-two years. I was devastated.

My life took such a sharp turn in a short period of time; I went from being a man who had a physically active job and enjoyed cycling twenty-five miles on a summer evening, to a man who may never walk again. I can't put into words how that felt. I was told I was always going to have this pain. It was a lot to take in all at once and I slipped into depression. One thought kept spiralling around my head; 'Why me?'

Each day felt like a struggle, fighting the pain and depression, but soon I had to face a new battle: my finances. The sudden drop in our income as a result of me being unable to work was difficult to manage. Each month was really tight and we often slipped behind with our bills. I always made sure the boys had enough food, but I often went without. To be honest, when you are going through depression and fear, you don't feel like eating anyway. It's the last thing you think about.

It didn't help that the TV constantly bombarded us with new things to buy. There were always new toys that the boys wanted, or they would come home from school and tell us about how all their friends were wearing the branded trainers or had fancy haircuts. It broke my heart at Christmas when they would say, 'My friend is getting this,' but we couldn't afford it. I can't blame them for asking, it's what any kid would do. We tried to shield our problems from them as much as we could; they were too young to understand. It wasn't because we didn't want to get them nice things, we just couldn't.

We could only afford the cheapest of the cheap, but at school the kids had to be wearing the latest shoes or jumpers, otherwise they didn't fit in. You can tell the people living on the breadline because of the clothes they wear. It got to a stage where we couldn't even buy the cheap trainers or plimsolls from the supermarket. Anyone who has young boys will know how quickly they go through trousers or shoes. If we had to buy new shoes one month, that would put us under. I felt like I had failed as a parent.

Falling behind with bill payments put a lot of stress on my marriage. We would argue all the time about money and I still had a lot of medical problems, which added to the pressure. The situation was slipping rapidly out of control and I decided to contact a debt management agency. Finally I thought we would get things sorted, but instead they made a complete mess of everything. They would pay bills that had already been paid and not others that needed to be sorted. Creditors would bombard me with calls, forcing me to try and negotiate with them, but I kept finding myself back at square one. The people who were meant to be helping were making things much worse. I was stressed and desperately suicidal as my debt continued to build up.

When you fall on hard times, it's devastating to realise that the people you thought were friends are nowhere to be found. I felt alone in my debt and began to withdraw into myself. My wife watched on helplessly as the distance grew between us. She knew I wasn't coping and she was so worried. She tried her best to keep me going, to keep the house going and protect my sons. I blamed everything on myself and neglected to see how much pressure I had put on her. Through it all, she was the glue that held the family together. She was the rock that I was clinging to.

I lived in constant fear, waiting for the postman to arrive and wondering what final demands and threats he would post through the letterbox. No post on Sunday brought some release, but there was no respite from the phone that constantly harassed me. I was terrified that bailiffs would come knocking at any time to take our stuff away. It was like living on a knife-edge. I had no peace at all. The chronic pain had already pushed me into depression, but the debt forced me further and further towards my wits' end. It all got too much; I had a nervous breakdown and tried to commit suicide.

It was through friends that I heard about CAP. I didn't call at first; I was too focused on the turmoil my life was in. I couldn't think straight and the last thing I wanted to do was admit that I needed help. To me, that meant I had failed and it went against everything I had been taught growing up. In the end, my friends sat me down, pushed a phone into my hand and made me call CAP. I was apprehensive, embarrassed and ashamed to lay my life open to Jean, the Centre Manager, but she had such a calming influence.

Jean turned up with another CAP volunteer and two big bags of shopping for the boys. I was staggered. With gentleness and sincerity, she explained who CAP was, how they could help and what we would need to do. She told us it was a team effort; CAP could help take everything off of us and would be there to deal with all the problems, provided we did our part. I was a little dubious, especially because of the bad experience I had with the previous debt management agency, but Jean took the fear away. I decided to trust them.

Jean told me that we would work together, but in the meantime I might still get calls. Now though, I just had to tell them to contact CAP instead of me and, in time, the number of calls would start to drop. It was a great relief knowing that CAP had taken over and that Jean would be on the end of the phone if we needed any help. The calls stopped after CAP negotiated on my behalf, and I no longer panicked over the letters. The pressure eased once CAP set us a budget that was liveable. There was enough money for food and to get clothes and shoes for the boys. We even had a savings account – it was outstanding.

Through the budget and the savings I was able to get a car, which gave me back my independence. I was able to get lessons from my father-in-law who is a driving instructor, and I made sure we put money aside for the MOT and tax. The accident had already robbed me of a lot of mobility; I can only walk short distances and climbing stairs gives me a lot of pain. The car was vital in giving me the freedom I needed to be able to go out and about, and take my family places. I lifted my head and began to win the fight against my depression.

Simple things meant a lot to me, like the bags of shopping or the calls from Findlay Church to see how I was. I was surprised at first, thinking they wanted something from me, but they simply wanted to help. It was the first time I had really seen people who were truly living out the Christian faith. I had never believed in God. I came from a family who let me believe what I wanted and it was up to me to make my own path. So I chose to be an agnostic, but later thought that was a cop out and became a staunch atheist. I wanted to see real evidence and thought the church was about someone telling you what to do and how bad you are. Then I saw people like Jean and others from church really living out the Christian message. It was a revelation to me and I began to re-evaluate my faith. I would joke with my friends about how I was an atheist, now I was joking that I had doubts about my doubts!

At first, it was my boys who wanted to go to Sunday school. They had been to a summer club that the church had put on and wanted to keep going. My wife was also interested in exploring faith and asked me to come along to church to support her. I agreed, 'But if they preach at me,' I said, 'I'll give them both barrels!'

I had heard that church attendance in the UK was falling and it was full of pensioners, but I was surprised when I arrived at this church to find people queuing to get in! As I walked through the door, I was stunned. The fellowship was vibrant and friendly and nothing like what I had expected. I kept my guard up, ready to respond with atheist arguments to anybody that dared to talk to me, but when I heard readings from the Bible, I realised just how wrong I was.

It was truly an eye opening experience. I realised that I actually had no evidence to prove that God didn't exist. I had seen for myself that Jesus lived in the people around me. A friend then read the parable about the prodigal son to me. It is about a father who gives his two sons his inheritance before he dies; but the younger son goes off and wastes it all. There is a famine, so the son returns home to beg his father's forgiveness. Instead of disowning him, the father welcomes him back with open arms, which makes the older son really angry. I took the viewpoint of the older son at first, but then I realised that it was all about grace. That was a real light-bulb moment; I was the prodigal son and I needed God's grace. From that moment, my life started to change.

I got really involved with church and was baptised. My wife also became a Christian; she took a little more time than me because she wanted to be really sure for herself. She was baptised too and our faith has strengthened our relationship in a big way. Together, we have moved forward and now I put my trust totally in God. My whole outlook on life has changed and instead of thinking, 'Why me?' I began to think, 'Why not me?' When I had my accident, I was very negative. It's like a grey cloud would come over me and I would see things in dark colours. Now I look for the positive in situations. Despite the bad, I can see how God has brought good things in my life. Because of my accident, for example, I am able to spend time with my boys and watch them grow up. Before, I would be working fourteen-hour shifts and weekends, only seeing them as they were tucked up in bed. Now we can go out and spend time together as a family.

Now I am doing things I never believed I would do, like leading worship. I played guitar a long time ago, but had to give it up, as it was too painful to hold with my injuries. When I had my breakdown, I was encouraged by the Glasgow mental health organisation to play it again to help with my recovery. I had to retrain myself to play in a new way and used to just strum to myself. Since coming to faith, the church found out about my playing and asked me to lead worship! I'd never have had the confidence to stand up in front of so many people, but I realised that it didn't matter because it was all for the Lord. Now I play in a band too, something that I have always wanted to do. I am living out my dreams. I couldn't have done it without him.

In September last year, we got the call to say that we were debt free. At first, I didn't believe it, but then as it sank in, I felt overwhelming relief. I had been with CAP for three years and wouldn't be here today without them. I still struggle with my back and can only walk short distances, but my car gives me freedom to get around and take the boys out. It was the budget set out by CAP that gave me that freedom. I also see it as a community resource and joke that I am the church taxi service. As I can't work, I am free to help others, taking them shopping or to hospital appointments.

Unfortunately, I do still suffer from depression as a side effect from the injury. Chronic pain and depression feed off each other, so I still get dark periods. But now I know I can take the way I am feeling to the Lord. I have real friends at church who stand by me and talk me through it. God has given me insight into other people's pain. I can sympathise with others and tell them they are not alone. It is a real comfort for people to know that. I understand how people feel when they are in debt and can relate. I tell them they are not a failure – sometimes the system just lets you down.

I felt CAP was so good to me and helped me so much that I wanted to give back and help them. I started to volunteer to help Jean by sharing my story with others. I know how people feel in these situations and if my story can help people and bring them forward, then I want to tell it. I believe God has been good to me and I want to pass it on. The message I have to tell people is one of hope. CAP gave me hope. I took a few steps and they walked alongside me. They certainly led me to faith, and the Christian faith is the full meaning of hope. I tell people to always remember there is hope. CAP might just be the beginning of that journey.

The first time I shared my story with others, Jean read out a piece of scripture from the Bible first: 'Is not this the kind of fasting I have chosen: to loose the chains of injustice and untie the cords of the yoke, to set the oppressed free and break every yoke? Is it not to share your food with the hungry and to provide the poor wanderer with shelter – when you see the naked, to clothe them, and not to turn away from your own flesh and blood?' (Isaiah 58:6-7)

For me, this is what CAP have done. They have broken the yoke by taking the burden of debt from around my neck. The ropes have been cut and now, life is freedom.

Healed

Katie Johnson

She just kept banging on about Jesus. Every morning when I arrived to care for her, she'd say, 'thank you Jesus for Katie'. Why was she thankful? If Jesus was so good, Libby wouldn't need me to turn up and look after her. She was in constant pain from cerebral palsy and confined to a wheelchair, but she was always smiling. I've always worked as a carer, but I've never looked after anyone like this. I suppose you could say it got me thinking. She kept asking me to go to church, so when she died, I decided to honour that and go. I could do that, at least.

As a carer, you forget about the other people that work with the same patient. Libby had ten of us in total, a mixture of other carers and support workers. Eight of them were Christians, but they didn't all start out that way. I guess she banged on about Jesus to them too and they must have done what she asked and gone to church. Just two of us were too stubborn then. If God loved her, why did he kill her? She wasn't old, so why did he allow her to suffer?

I'd been to church as a kid. I was in the choir and played the harp like a little angel. My dad always made us go, which was odd considering he didn't come with us and wasn't a Christian. Maybe it was just a generational thing, or he thought it would make us good – teach us morals or something. A lady, Brenda, used to look after me and my brother and sisters at a youth club called Crusaders at church. She'd take us for tea at her house afterwards and tell us stories about Jesus. I wondered why she bothered; he didn't really exist, did he?

* * *

It was 2003, a year after getting married and starting work as a carer, when I went along to church again. The people were so nice, and I went with a friend and enjoyed her company. But for five years, as I attended every week and sat through every talk and song, I still felt like I didn't belong, yet had a sense that I needed to be there. After two years, I was on the Parish Church Council and working with the children's summer clubs. I'd even been baptised, which was odd, seeing as I didn't really believe it was all true. I still wasn't sure about God and really didn't believe what Christians thought about Jesus.

After three years, my husband and I moved house and I decided to look for a local church. There were three churches in my village, but the first one I tried was closed the morning I went. The leaders were there, however, and they suggested I come back next week and try them out. They were lovely; even when I told them I didn't believe in Jesus and didn't read my Bible, because to me it was outdated and boring. It didn't seem to faze them. In fact, they told me they had been praying for a new family to come to the church, and were delighted that I was there with my two children.

I kept going though. I loved how kind everyone was. No one judged me; everyone simply wanted me to be me. You see, I wanted my kids to have the same Sunday School experience I'd had with Brenda at Crusaders. Like my dad, my husband stayed at home; he'd 'done' church as a boy, been confirmed and all that jazz, and he simply didn't feel he needed church or that church needed him. One Sunday however, my church leader, Mick, asked if we would like to come camping with the church to an event called Grapevine. It was five days away that we really needed; we were in debt and it would be a welcome break for us as a family. We were on a debt management plan, which didn't leave a lot for holidays, so we decided to go. However, my husband was less than enthusiastic about being around so many Christians all at once (sandals and socks came to mind!).

On the second day, this guy got up and started talking about struggling to feed his kids because of debt. As I listened, I was so inspired by all that he had overcome. He said he had started a charity called Christians Against Poverty (CAP) and I just knew I wanted to be involved. I used to work for Citizens Advice, but stopped when I had kids. I told my church that we had to open a CAP Debt Centre, but they said that I couldn't be the Centre Manager because I wasn't a Christian. I was so annoyed. 'They won't know', I thought, 'Jesus isn't real, it's just a nice story'. I still struggled to understand how God could even exist with all the things that had happened to me.

Now this guy, John Kirkby, was talking about something I really believed I could do, and do well. Also, I had experience in this stuff; I knew what the burden of debt felt like. My husband and I were in the process of paying off over £50,000 of debt.

It had started off with just small things like overdrafts and loans left over from our university days, and then we took out a loan to buy our first house and furnish it. But then several things happened that same year and our finances slipped quickly out of control.

Both my dad and Libby (the reason I went to church) passed away and, after falling pregnant with our first child, I unexpectedly lost both my jobs. Work had told me that they just couldn't insure me whilst I was pregnant, so I found work as a self-employed Kleeneze distributor. It wasn't enough money to live off at first and, naively, we lived off credit cards for quite a few months. Then things started to look up again just three months after baby number two was born, so we bought a new house. With our outgoings just matching our income, we tried to furnish the new house with credit cards. With cards to pay off and a loan that had massively increased to support the new mortgage, it wasn't long before our debts escalated. At one point we had twelve credit and store cards and two bank accounts with full overdrafts.

I went to get some advice about our debts, but being self-employed, it wasn't straightforward to budget our money. When we put together a debt recovery plan, I was disheartened to hear it could take up to seventeen years to pay all our debts off! Still, we were adamant that we would honour our debts, so we refused to go bankrupt, and instead increased our income where we could and agreed that we would pay them off despite how long it took. I could relate first-hand to the experience of others dealing with debts and so I really connected with what John was saying.

The following day, during another service at Grapevine, a man called Dwayne Wright was talking about building churches in run down towns and cities, and I sat there thinking, 'That would be amazing, everyone being kind to each other, just like at my church'. We sang a song that said, 'greater things are yet to come, greater things are still to be done in this city'. That was it. I knew I wanted to 'do CAP' with all my heart, but I couldn't get past the 'Jesus died for me' thing. I was an idiot who had made a ton of mistakes in my life, some never to be discussed with anyone. He wouldn't die for me – I wasn't worth it.

During that song, I spoke to God. I said, 'Okay, if you are real, get yourself down here and prove it'. He answered. In an instant, I was overwhelmed with his presence and I knew he was real. I still had questions, but there was no getting away from him. While everyone was singing, I was shouting, 'There is a Jesus!' My church were with me and they just laughed – they had been telling me that for a while. That night, I had a dream about running a CAP Debt Centre. I knew it was from God.

After the meeting, I had to tell my husband, Mark, about it. I must have made an impression, or at least been enthusiastic, as he agreed to come to the meeting the next day. He had been to a previous meeting, but it seemed to make him cry and so he had decided not to go back. However, he did come to the next meeting and he became a Christian as well. Now my whole family was heading in the right direction!

The next step was to read my Bible. It said in the book they gave us when we became Christians that we should read it, but I couldn't understand why. As much as I tried in the past, it was too hard to understand and despite my perseverance, it was just so boring! People kept telling me to 'start here', or 'read it in this order', but it never worked. If God wanted me to read the Bible, he could come down and tell me himself. The next day (still at camp), he decided to let me know his opinion on the subject. The speaker's talk was called, 'Why you should read the Bible for all you are worth.' It was all about the importance of reading the Bible if you wanted to grow as a Christian – I now needed a Bible and my wonderful church went out and bought me one at camp. I started reading that night and now no one can stop me. In the front of my new Bible, Mick's wife, Deb, had written a verse from Hebrews: 'Jesus Christ is the same yesterday and today and forever' (Hebrews 13:8). It's a verse that I have never forgotten.

So here I was, a new Christian, fresh off the block and told by God that I would run a CAP Debt Centre. The church had been praying for someone to run it, but I don't think they thought it would be me! Eager to pursue the vision God had given me for a debt centre, we called CAP and registered for a Church Partnership Day at their head office in Bradford. The day was put on for churches that were interested in finding out more about the work of CAP and how they might partner with them. So in late 2008, as I walked around Jubilee Mill, I felt really excited about the idea of bringing CAP into my local community. However, my bubble of enthusiasm was burst in an instant when they told me, 'Sorry Katie, but your church is too small'.

With a humble congregation of just twenty, we are a small church, but God had richly blessed us to be a close-knit family that has an incredible way of loving each other. We call it a 'hospital church', because of all the incredible healings we've seen and we are able to support and nurture people in a way we couldn't if we were much bigger. God is so good, I just knew that the size of the church didn't matter, but despite my best efforts to convince CAP otherwise, they told me they just weren't in a position to be able to partner at that point in time. I sat there and sobbed – I couldn't understand why God had shut the door after speaking so clearly before.

Just then, one of the CAP team gave me a ray of hope; he told me that I could go away and run the CAP Money Course through my church instead. Perhaps if I came back in a few years they might look again at a CAP Debt Centre. I grasped the opportunity with both hands and set out to run this as well as I could. Determined not to give up hope of one day opening a debt centre, I ripped off my delegate name badge from the day, wrote the year 2008 and scribbled underneath my name 'Debt Coach' and stuck it to my 'goals' board at home. In 2010, whilst at leadership training, we had to prepare a talk about our vision for our ministry, and I prepared a talk about the CAP Debt Centre I intended to run by 2015. 'They can't say no forever!' I concluded. Afterwards, I pinned the talk underneath the badge on the goals board.

Once I was back home, I immediately began to put the CAP Money Course into practice for our finances. As soon as we began to put the

CAP Money Course principles to use, we were amazed to find that we could save £400 a month. It was incredible; no one ever told us to write down and work out where to save, spend and cut back like that. We went through everything and cut out stuff we knew we didn't need. The £400 made a massive difference and suddenly we were able to shave four years off the plan to clear our debts. I closed the bank accounts and took all my cards and pinned them on the goal board at home; once our debts were clear I would move them to the achievements board as a reminder that I would never let that happen again.

So in 2009, we started running CAP Money Courses and then I found out I was pregnant with our third child. It was like a gift from God, we were so excited. Then at twenty weeks, when I was just thirty-one, I started fainting and feeling very poorly. I was asked to wear a twenty-four hour monitor to ascertain what was wrong, if anything. It was meant to put my mind at rest. Instead, I had to rush into hospital, twenty-three weeks pregnant. I was scared for my life and for the life of my baby. It turned out I have an AV block, which means the bottom part of my heart stops occasionally. I had to have a pacemaker fitted immediately.

I was beyond scared. I actually called Mick and Deb before my husband and asked them to pray for me. I thought I couldn't be that sick; I was a Christian now! Mick was fantastic and stayed on the phone whilst I called my husband to ask him to come home and take me to the hospital immediately as I needed surgery. It was surreal. During surgery, I couldn't be sedated, as it would put my baby at further risk. The doctors had already told me everything that could go wrong so I was terrified. I lay still for nearly an hour while a pacemaker was inserted into my body and two wires were put into my heart. I remember thinking I was going to die; this was it. I prayed like mad. I asked Jesus to come and comfort me and there he was, at the end of my bed. I slowly chanted Psalm 23, 'the Lord is my shepherd, I shall not want...' and hung on to the hope that it was all in God's hands; he had sent the doctors and I would put all my trust in him and them. Prayer is awesome – I was released from hospital just hours after the operation.

Five months later, when my third child was born, the wires from my pacemaker pulled a little hole in my heart and a litre of blood had pooled around the area. I wasn't aware until I collapsed on the morning of my little girl's birthday. I was rushed to hospital; the doctors had no idea what was wrong. I couldn't eat and was getting weaker and weaker. Then the blackouts and seizures started. My husband and I began to fear the worse. I prayed like mad; I wanted to see my children grow up. My baby boy was only five weeks old and my other son had just turned five.

Shocked, scared and very aware it was my daughter's seventh birthday, I didn't want mummy dying to be her lasting memory. I told God that I knew he could heal all things and asked that if it wasn't in his plan to heal me, to please love and look after my three children and my husband. In that moment, I lost all fear of death and truly believed that there was a God. I knew that he was good, even through it all. You see, I had nowhere else to turn, no rock other than him to cling to. My husband was not in the room, I was surrounded by doctors, I was barely conscious, but I felt warm and at peace. 'Whom else is there but God?' I asked myself.

I was told it would take six weeks of antibiotics to heal me enough to go home and that I may have continuing heart problems, but I was home and healed six days after being rushed in! No long term damage, no continuing problems. Boy, can my church pray! I was only in hospital for six days, yet it seemed like nearly every one of them who was able, visited and prayed with me or for my family and me.

Looking back, it seems odd that I would be reading Psalms from the Bible aloud whilst I was there. I know how it started; I was just reading from my Bible on the first day in hospital, when a doctor mentioned Psalm 73:26: 'My flesh and my heart may fail, but God is the strength of my heart and my portion for ever'. As I was talking, he suddenly stopped me. 'I think we've prayed for you', he said. It turned out he knew Brenda, the lady who used to take me to Crusaders, so long ago. They were in a church small group together. Now my doctor could tell her that her prayers had been answered, I had found the Lord and let him into my life. After that, it just happened every day at the same time after visiting. I would read my Bible aloud and the lovely ladies on the beds around me would ask me to read out their favourite Psalm. It was like having my own radio programme. The nurses would even stop and listen from time to time. With everything going on, people must have looked on and wondered how I stayed a Christian. I made some good friends in the hospital though and we stayed in touch to give each other hope.

My little girl's eighth birthday rolled round and I was taken into surgery again, this time with a rare cervical cancer. For the third time in just eighteen months, I was faced with the very real thought that I may never see my children grow up; that it was not what God had planned for me. But I was given a verse by Deb: "'For I know the plans I have for you,' declares the LORD, 'plans to prosper you and not to harm you, plans to give you hope and a future.'" (Jeremiah 29:11). Mark and I spoke to the children, and we explained to Lauren that mummy would be in the hospital again on her birthday, but she could visit me and have a day off of school. 'Wouldn't that be fun?' I said.

Surgery day came, and there was another couple with us, whom we had met during our pre-op visits. She had stage four cancer and had already had many organs removed to try to stem the growth. We asked if we could pray for her and her husband, and they agreed. When I came around from surgery, very groggy, the lady was waiting by my bedside. Still very ill as I was, she whispered that my prayers had worked, and the cancer had not spread any further and she could go home. I don't even know if I answered her, as I had lost too much blood during surgery and needed an urgent blood transfusion. I pray that she went to church and gave her life to God after that day, but I don't know if she did.

Two days later, my daughter's birthday, and I was just able to stand. On my way to the day room to meet her, I collapsed in a pool of blood. The next thing I remember, as I was rushed back to surgery, was shouting not to let my children out of the room so they didn't see me like that. I went into anaphylactic shock during recovery and had to be sedated and put on a ventilator in the Intensive Care Unit. It was a scary time, but even then, God didn't leave me. I had another frank conversation with God. I needed him to do something. I just challenged him to get on with it. If I was staying, then fix me, but if I was going to die then don't hang around; just get on with it. I was in so much pain and I could barely see. I like that God is big enough for those kinds of conversations. He is my dad – he knows how he made me and is happy to talk with me, however he finds me. And he found me pretty cross that day. My church prayed, even my mother prayed (who now comes to church), and all in all I was only in hospital six days, released just forty-eight hours after coming off the ventilator and just in time for Christmas. God is awesome.

In March 2011, I was recovering from the cancer when I went to a CAP event for churches running the CAP Money Course. It was announced that CAP had found a way to partner with smaller churches, which meant our church could open a CAP Debt Centre! After completing the Centre Manager training at CAP's head office, I took my delegate name badge, added the year (2011) and proudly pinned it to my 'achievements' board, alongside the goals board where I had stuck the previous badge two years ago. It was all in God's perfect timing. Three near deaths experiences in three years – I truly understood God's power that can never be shaken. Boy does that guy know what he's doing!

Working for CAP is all I hoped it would be and more. I have spent all my life caring for people. It is just something God put in me. I could love and look after people all day. And now, God has given me a place where I can do it all day for his purpose. The love CAP shows to clients and the service I am able to offer through them is phenomenal. There is nothing else like it. I have been a nurse, a care assistant and a carer and these all gave me great experience for the work I do now. At CAP, we get to go beyond paperwork and logistics and interact with the people. I'm not behind my desk, but next to them on their sofa.

After all I have been through, I know that no matter what problems are placed in front of me, when I walk through a client's door, I will have already been through it: debt, illness, grief. Just the other day, I was able to block out a whole day to sit with one of my clients who had been diagnosed with cancer. I know that whatever someone is going through, they can look at me and see that it is possible to smile again. They know that there is a way out. Taking God's love and the hope he offers through his work at CAP, and through the local church, really does transform people's lives.

It has been a mad journey and I wouldn't have believed you if you had told me all that I would go through, but God has been with me and has guided me through the whole thing. I would have said up until that point, my biggest fear in life would have to be death – death for me and for my children. Now I have such hope, death is just the next step on the journey to be with my God and it will never scare me again. If God brings me to it, he will bring me through it. Amen.

Reconciled

Alan & Jeani Day

'What's wrong, Jeani?' Angelina asked, crouching down beside me to smooth a comforting hand across my back. Her gentle words were too much and I broke down, leaning forward and burying my head in my hands. Angelina waited patiently as I fought back the tears to answer her question. Slowly the words come out between uncontrollable sobs; 'I…have…left…Alan,' I said.

Alan and I had just had another huge row about money when I walked out. I ended up in the town centre because it was the first place my feet took me, but now I wasn't sure what to do. I couldn't think straight and found myself wandering aimlessly, looking in shop windows as though I would find an answer behind their glassy frames. I found only hopelessness, and sat down, staring into the blur of people around me. I must have looked terrible because my friend had spotted me from a nearby shop and rushed over to see what was the matter.

My phone rang and without hesitation I looked straight at my friend and said sternly, 'I don't want to talk to him.' I knew it was Alan without checking; he had been calling and texting ever since I left. 'You should go home, Jeani,' my friend pleaded, 'he will be worried sick.' I shook my head. I couldn't bear the thought of going back.

She took me to her house, pleading with me all the way to call him and go home, but I was adamant. Alan was the last person I wanted to talk to. I wondered what words we could say that wouldn't lead to a fight. Our money situation was getting worse and we were on the verge of losing the house. Neither of us knew what to do. In the end I agreed to call my daughter to let her know I was safe, but I made no promises to come home.

Alan

I got the text from Jeani saying she wasn't coming home and I stared at the words for a long time. My relief at knowing she was safe turned to desperation and despair as I dialled the number again and again, and sent text messages with no reply. I managed to find where she was through one of her friends, and I hoped that she might persuade Jeani to come home, but it was useless. I was shocked; I didn't know how things had got so bad. I just didn't know what to do.

Our financial problems started when I had an accident at work. I worked as a carpet fitter but work was scarce, so I decided to apply for some part time hours to keep us going. I quickly snapped up a cleaning job at a hotel. It was going well, until one day I slipped in the kitchen and broke my hip. It was a nasty break which led to an operation to fit screws to hold it in place. I was forced to leave work for much longer than I had expected in order to recover.

After eighteen months, I couldn't believe it when the doctors told me that the bones still hadn't healed properly. They decided I would need a second operation, but this time I would need a full hip replacement. The idea of going back to work any time soon faded away and a wave of disappointment came over me. It was already a financial burden that I had been out of work this long and I started to worry about how we would manage. I felt like I had let Jeani down.

At the same time, my shoulder had been giving me a lot of pain. I think I damaged it when I fell, but I dismissed it at first because my hip was the main concern. However, the pain had gradually been getting worse and now I couldn't ignore it any longer. After an examination, the doctors explained it was caused by the bone rubbing against the muscle and that I would need surgery on that too. If that wasn't enough, in between these surgeries, I had a further two operations to remove cataracts from my eyes. I felt bitter at being stuck in the hospital when all I wanted was to be out earning a living and providing for my family.

It was a really difficult time for me and, to make matters worse, I didn't receive any compensation for my accident, despite it not being my fault. It was a lot to take on board all at once and the loss in my income hit us hard. We couldn't keep up with our bills and mortgage, and it was scary how quickly things spiralled out of control. We tried to cut back, but things got desperate and it looked like we might lose the house. That's when Jeani walked out.

Jeani

The day I left home, life wasn't worth living. I kept thinking, 'How are we going to get out of this?' There was no light at the end of the tunnel, no solution to pursue. We were both without a job and quickly slipped behind with mortgage payments. Credit cards were left unpaid, the bills and demands building up to the point where we'd skip meals to pay them. It was really tough.

Alan was already struggling after his accident and, with all the worry about money, I joined him in his depression. We argued all the time and I would always end up shouting at him and the kids. My blood pressure increased, due to the stress. One day, it got too much. I walked out. I couldn't take it anymore. I just needed to get out and be on my own. That's when Angelina found me and convinced me to call my daughter.

After calling, I went over to see her and told her everything. 'Why on earth didn't you tell us, Mum?' she said. I don't really know how it had got so bad, but around the time when Alan was off work because of his accident, my daughter was diagnosed with a brain tumour. My grandson had problems with his legs, so I had also given up work to look after them both. I did what any mother would do. I felt bad, but I had just wanted to protect her. She had enough going on in her life and I thought that telling her would just add to her stress. It was enough for Alan and I without involving anyone else.

Looking back, I realise we should have told people sooner, but when you are in debt, you feel like you need to sort it out yourself. You think perhaps you can manage alone if you just keep trying a little bit longer. We tried and it didn't work. However, help came when a friend put me in touch with a solicitor. The solicitor worked at the same place as the husband of Fiona Bruce MP. I called up and blurted everything out. After explaining my situation, he said calmly, 'I know just the sort of people who can help you.' Determined, I called Alan and told him that we were going to get help.

Alan

It was a huge relief when Jeani called to say that we were going to get things sorted. I was glad to know she would be coming home. She told me that people from an organisation called 'CAP' were going to come and see us. She didn't tell me much about them other than they help people in debt. I wasn't sure if they could help us but I was out of other ideas.

I was sceptical when Steve from Christians Against Poverty stepped into our home. He told us how CAP works and that they were a Christian organisation, and I wondered what we were getting ourselves into. I wasn't religious and I was worried that they might make us go to church. I needn't have worried – there was never any pressure to do religious stuff, and Steve explained that his faith was the reason behind the charity and not in any way a prerequisite for clients to receive help.

We talked for a long time about our situation. It felt good to finally tell someone about everything, as Jeani and I had kept it secret from everyone else for so long. I handed over piles and piles of bills and letters, and it was like someone pulling a plug and letting all the stress and pressure drain away. He was so calm and compassionate as we shared everything we'd been through. He genuinely wanted to help us and, at first, I couldn't understand why he would care.

The second time he came over, he brought a couple with him. They were CAP volunteers who offered their support to Jeani and I. That very evening they offered to take us out for a meal. We were really surprised by their kindness but were grateful, as we hadn't had a decent meal in a very long time. We had a wonderful time and it was great to go out and leave our worries at home for a while. They continued to keep in touch and often took us out for coffee and food. They were always there when we needed someone to talk to and we have since become really good friends. They were supportive, just like Steve was, without wanting anything in return.

The phone calls from creditors, which were a constant chorus before, stopped. We didn't fear the letters that came through the door, knowing that we could just send them on to CAP. We knew that another compassionate person in CAP's head office was working behind the scenes, fighting our corner and sorting everything out. We didn't have to worry any more.

Jeani

I hadn't told Alan what CAP stood for because I was worried he wouldn't be interested if he thought they were religious. I thought I would get away with just referring to them as 'CAP' the whole time until Steve came around to visit. The first thing he said when he opened the door was, 'Hi, I'm Steve from Christians Against Poverty.' I wanted the ground to open up. Alan was stood next to me and I thought, 'Oh no! He's going to kick him out!' Fortunately, Steve explained that whilst they are a Christian charity, they help anyone regardless of what they believe and that there was no pressure. I looked at Alan and he looked a little sceptical but breathed a sigh of relief as he welcomed Steve into the lounge.

We sat down together and Steve played a DVD with people on it who had been through exactly what we were going through. I watched with tear-filled eyes as people shared how debt made them feel and that they were now debt free. For the first time, I felt like there was some hope for us. I told Steve that what CAP had done for these people was wonderful and that I wanted that too. Alan agreed to give it a go. That night after Steve left was the best night's sleep we'd had in ages!

A week or so later we got a call from Steve saying he was going to come over and take us food shopping. I was really taken back, but we went along as he took us to the supermarket. I was so overwhelmed; I remember just sitting in the car at Tesco crying as he bought us all this food - I couldn't believe it. CAP have been fantastic, helping us the way they do.

Although Steve had always said to us that we didn't have to go to church, I really wanted to. He offered to come pick us up because we had no transport. As we got into the car he said, 'If you don't like it, that's okay', but I remember that, as soon as I walked through the door, I was absolutely blown away. I had been to other churches before, but this one was very different. People were so happy and friendly and invited me in with open arms. I felt right at home and quickly got involved with the Foodbank and volunteering at church. I decided

to get baptised on Palm Sunday and commit my life entirely to Jesus –
it was a wonderful service.

Alan

When Jeani told me she had become a Christian, I didn't believe in God,
but I was happy to go along to church together. I hadn't been in a church
for over fifty years but the people there were great and we were welcomed
like family.

Then in August, CAP took us away on holiday. It was a short break
away with other couples, families and individuals who were also in debt.
I was amazed at how many others were in similar circumstances to us.
I had never thought about it before; when you are in debt you think
you are all on your own. It was good to talk to other people and relate
to what each other were going through. It was great to get away and
spend time together as a couple without arguing about money.

Whilst I was there, I talked to a man named David who worked
for CAP in Leicester. We talked about God and I explained how I felt.
I knew that Jeani had made a decision but I needed something more;
I wanted confirmation that God was there. David offered to pray for
me and I agreed, thinking I didn't have anything to lose. He said,
'Lord, please give Alan a sign that only he will understand.'

I thought nothing more about it and went back to enjoying the holiday.
The next day, after we had been to a safari park, one of the ladies gave
a talk about her life and how she found God. She was about the same
age as me and I could relate to what she was saying. It moved me in a
way I had never felt before. Afterwards, she said if anyone wanted to ask
God into their life, then we could pray a prayer of salvation. As she told
everyone to close their eyes, all of a sudden, I put my hand up. A man

called Rod came over and I repeated the salvation prayer after him. Jeani was sat next to me – she couldn't believe it!

Later on, as we were packing up to go home, I saw David again and I told him what had happened. He said to me, 'Do you realise what just happened? It's the sign!' It gave me a kick to go back to church. I started making cakes for everyone, and now they call me 'Mr K', after Mr Kipling!

Whilst working with CAP, we also had the opportunity to have a tour of Jubilee Mill, which is CAP's head office in Bradford. It was amazing to meet John Kirkby and hear his story of what he had been through. I remember walking around the mill and seeing all the staff smiling and happy. I thought they were actors.

'Are these people real?' I asked John.

'Yeah, they are proper people!' he replied.

Jeani

CAP has been absolutely marvellous. We didn't know that there were people like this in the world. It has completely changed my life and people have seen a complete transformation in me. Things are by no means perfect and life is still really tough. We are in the process of losing the house because of going through bankruptcy, but I won't let it get me down. Now when things are tough, I know I have God on my side.

God steps in

Claire Page

A piece of bread for lunch again. It will be enough, I'm used to it now. I can't remember the last time I had a real sandwich. I've had to leave my job. The tiredness, feeling ill all the time, constant pain in my joints. Could I be dying? It's scary when you are tired, ill and in pain, not knowing why. I could just end it. I mean really. I don't have my job anymore. I can't eat properly, can't tell anyone. The stress is getting too much and the debt is still mounting up. Without work it is going to be impossible to pay it back.

I fell up the stairs the other day. That made my knees even worse. That's just something else to think about. It was hard enough to think about my debts while I was at work, but now with this constant tiredness and pain, I just can't focus on them – not that I have the money to pay them anyway. I feel so low – I really can't see a way out, the wall of debt is so high. Suicide is playing on my mind, big time.

I miss my job. It was long hours and no weekends, but I could pay my debts and buy nice things. But Christmas is coming up and I'll still have to buy everyone some big presents. It's probably my last one though – why worry about what I spend? Go out with a bang instead. I'm worried sick and thinking ahead just gets me more upset. I don't know why. The headaches are getting worse too. What's the point of eating properly? I'm not going to be here for long anyway. The GP did some tests and took some fluid. He sent them to the hospital. I'm not sure I want the results back.

Well, Christmas came and went, and now my test results have come back. Rheumatoid arthritis, no cure. I'm horrified and want to die; after all, I thought I would. It is the last thing I needed. My health just keeps going downhill with problem on top of problem: blood disorders, inhalers for breathing, steroid injections, painkillers, dry eyes, joints out of place and infections. Sad and confused doesn't begin to describe it. Yet I'm still here! But I spent way too much at Christmas – that's scary. I feel like I need to run for my life. I really need to do something about this. Maybe I can find something on the internet? I'll have a look for a debt website. This one looks different. And they have a free book...

* * *

That's when I found out about CAP and everything changed. Their book, Nevertheless, came really quickly. It was really inspiring reading all that John had overcome and the help they had given to clients. I was fascinated by how other people's lives had changed. I wanted to know who this Jesus was and how to get that change in my life – I needed it. Just from reading the book, I knew they wouldn't judge me or blame me, so I gave them a call. The lady who answered was lovely and she put me at ease straight away. It was strange at first to speak on the phone to somebody with a caring voice. There were no demands and no fear as I poured out my situation with desperation.

'Everything is going to be okay,' she said, 'there's a way out and we're going to help you.'

From that first phone call, I knew things were going to be okay. While I was waiting for my appointment, CAP sent through letters for me to pass on to the creditors that explained I was getting help with my debts. I felt different already.

I remember watching Di drive past my house. I was nervous. Butterflies had free rein in my stomach as I watched her walk up to the door, and I opened it to her smiling face. A wave of peace seemed to flow into the house and I realised I was smiling as well.

The first thing she said was, 'How are you doing?' No one ever asked me that – well, maybe doctors, but that was it. No one was ever concerned about me. So often, I was bullied. I kept people out, stood on my own. I certainly didn't trust people and I was scared to love – I might get hurt. But here was Di, a stranger, and she broke down my walls in an instant. She wasn't heartless like so many other people had been. With her, there was peace, trust and honesty straight away.

This was a breakthrough for me. I had to be honest. We sat down to go through my debts. I had to face my worst fears and declare all. She took time and infinite care as we looked at each debt one by one. She took them all without a single look of disappointment or a word of judgment. Linda, the Befriender who came with Di also really helped; she was so kind as we chatted through everything. I knew they were there to help and I believed them.

You could see that Di's heart was really pure. She clearly understood my debt problems, but more than that, she understood my health problems too. There was something different about her. It was the same hope and peace that John had talked about in Nevertheless and I could see it so clearly in Di. Nowadays I know what that is; I call her my 'God Lady'. I was still thinking about the change those other clients had experienced in the book and I wanted it too. I had always believed in God, but I wanted to know him. I could see that Di knew him on such a personal level and that it made all the difference for her.

Di was busy sorting out the debt – to be able to hand it over was brilliant – but to be honest, I was more interested in the idea of God and how to get that change for myself. As we went through my debts, Di chatted to me and really made me feel better. She lifted me back up. We then chatted about God and the book I had read. She said that if

I wanted that change for myself, there was a prayer that I could pray. We prayed a salvation prayer together and after that it was amazing! I felt so at peace.

It was then time for her to leave and I showed her to the door. After letting her out, I headed back to the living room and something very strange happened. The room was full of a big mist. At first I thought maybe dust had blown in and the sun was shining through it, but it was too different for that. It just floated there, beautiful and silent like the faintest cloud flecked with a million stars. Nothing on earth could have caused this kind of cloud. I felt so overjoyed with it. It felt so different. When I told Di, she said it was God. Apparently in the Bible it says that God sometimes appears as a cloud or mist; however, I had never known that before. It was in that moment that I knew I was doing the right thing and that was God's way of showing me he was there. It makes me smile even now, knowing that God came to visit me. He has become my best friend forever.

Another time when I was ill in bed with hot sweats, I phoned Di. She prayed for me over the phone and when I went down to the living room, the same mist was there again. When I went back to bed that night, I was fine. I will treasure the way God showed himself to me always.

A fortnight later, Di returned with my budget. She had already lifted a great weight from me when she took all my paperwork away. From that second visit, I just had to pay in the amount they asked; it was such a relief. There was never any pressure, but I trusted it was the best way. Yes it was hard, but I got on with it. And of course CAP helped. It meant I was able to get through it. I was able to talk to creditors with confidence because CAP was dealing with my debt. I would tell anyone else in debt that the best thing is to follow the CAP way. I did – I followed them completely, listened to them and did everything I needed to do. They put me on the right track. Everything was organised to perfection.

While all this was happening, Di and Linda never stopped looking after me. Through sad times, they were always there. They gave me food vouchers that really lifted the pressure of my food shop. I even got an amazing Christmas hamper, which made for such a different Christmas to the year before – which, at the time, I thought would be my last.

I felt totally different and the hamper was amazing. It had everything: chocolates, food for the cupboards, biscuits and crisps – really nice luxury things. The type of things I wouldn't have put in my trolley because of debt. This time, Christmas wasn't just a big bill and debt. This time it wasn't about presents. It was about people. I am learning that as I get to know the people at Life Spring Church.

I remember the first time I went there with Di. I could just feel that Jesus loved me when I was there. I still feel it every time I go. It is like his arms are around me. I am always filled with love and blessings there. Thanks to all my amazing friends at Life Spring – and Di and Linda's support – I can smile through my illness. I really enjoy helping out there and giving what I can to the church. It is great to be able to help. Even if money is tight, I never want to leave someone in need.

I even took my partner to the church. I just had to share it with him. He went on the Alpha Course. I prayed that Jesus would show his face; I was desperate for him to meet the God that had transformed my life. To his amazement, my partner saw God in the corner of church! I couldn't believe that Jesus had answered my prayer in such a powerful way – amazing! It's all part of the journey I started when I first found CAP's website. God has been with me through everything and it was all part of his plan.

Just before I went debt free, I got to visit CAP's Head Office in Bradford. Di and I went there, ate lunch and had a look around the building. We got to meet John, which was amazing, especially after reading his book. As we walked around, it was wonderful to see how all the staff were really busy and were helping so many thousands of people. All those people who depended on CAP; whose debts are in their hands.

I knew that everyone could be in a situation just like mine was, and I knew that they were all being given that glimmer of hope that was first shown to me when I made the call. I was truly grateful that my case was there. It was great to be able to thank them in person. They all do great work and are such amazing, caring people. I wasn't just another case to them; I was a person that needed love and support, and they gave it to me in abundance. It is so important that all the people out there in debt have someone who recognises that every case is different and is there to support them. I know that I was grateful they understood mine. After visiting CAP's offices, I knew that every single person who called was treated in the same way – with genuine compassion for their situation and a real desire to share the love of God.

Excitingly, I am now debt free thanks to a Debt Relief Order (DRO). This allowed me to become debt free, as I really couldn't afford to repay my debts – I'd still be facing impossible payments now. When I look back, I realise it didn't take CAP a very long time to deal with all my debts. I think back to my visit to CAP's headquarters, picture everyone and really understand what it meant to get me to where I am now. I have a real respect for what everyone did.

Now if I can't afford something, I don't get it. Sometimes, I go round town and every time I would have bought something, I write it down. These are all things that I don't need. That way, when I get home I can look at all the money I didn't spend, and feel proud of my better habits and changed attitude. I have faced up to what I had done in the past and dealt with it. Now I can start again, stress free; I will never get into debt again.

Looking at my life now, it is totally different – I am no longer suicidal. In a way, CAP and Di saved my life. She is an amazing lady and now my friend. I trust and believe in her and Linda. I know I can turn to them. There is such peace when I spend time with them. The amazing thing is that even though I am debt free, I know I have them to depend on.

It's been a year since I became a Christian and God has done lots of things. I have pictures and words, and I get healing when I go to church. I'm also part of Di's life group. God seems to speak to me through lots of hearts – I think it is to remind me that he loves me. You see, I am the type of person who feels I can love everyone in the world, but I really struggle to let anyone love me. Past bullying has played a big part in that and I have found it hard to trust what people say. Too many times, I have let people love me but they have hurt me.

The first heart appeared just as a picture when I closed my eyes before going to an Alpha meeting. It was so clear and then when I went upstairs to the meeting room I saw the same heart on the wall. It was the first time I saw it and it was exactly the same as the one I had seen in my mind. Then on Valentine's Day, when I was making pancakes, I turned one over to find a heart perfectly formed on the other side. In that moment, I was reminded of Jesus' love for me. There have been so many other incidents like this. Whilst I still struggle sometimes to believe God truly loves me, I know that with time that will change as he is healing me bit by bit.

The great thing is, I'm no longer scared of bullying, because I'm not alone. You can't imagine the difference that makes after a lifetime of being bullied in school and work. I remember chatting to Linda one day – I talk to her a lot – and I was talking to her about bullying. I was telling her that even though my health is so poor, bullying was still the worst thing I had faced in the past. I asked her what I should say if I saw a person who bullied me. She replied that I should tell them that Jesus loves them. Wow!

Now I know I can hold my head up. CAP showed me how valued I am, and showed me that there are honest, lovely people who want to help others. They never made me feel bad. With them, I was able to cry and tell the truth about my debt. They had care in their hearts, which meant I had no shame in mine for the debts I'd gotten myself into. They removed the stress from my life, which has given me the strength to build myself back up with God's help.

This means I have strength to face the pain that we all face in our lives. I know the thing is to keep going. I have come so far. The days are getting better and Di is there for the bad ones. Since I experienced God in my living room, I look forwards instead of at my past. I know that I can cope because God is for me. With each day I grow stronger. Before I was living at such a fast pace that I used to panic and get myself in a mess. But now I have learnt to slow life down, trust God and not worry so much.

I'm even looking at heading back to work now. I signed up to the Work Choice programme, which has helped me find a work placement suitable for my health issues. I have just passed accreditation and my assessors told me that they were really pleased with my hard work and determination.

I also received a letter from my placement company saying that they were so impressed with me, they would be keen to employ me once a post becomes available. In the meantime they are offering me some temporary work, which I hope to start soon. I showed Di the letter and she was really excited for me. It has given me a real confidence boost. All these things remind me that Jesus knows exactly what I need

I can honestly say that without God, CAP and my DRO, I wouldn't have got through everything. It has been a journey of care, love and support, and I have made lots of new friends. I have learnt a lot from taking the right path and sticking to all my CAP arrangements. Now I feel able to cope with money, which is amazing. In it all, Jesus gave me a peace that I have never in all my life felt before. And that peace has never left me.

Revived

Mary Jeevan

It started when my husband left, though really, he was never mine. I'd brought him over from India to England, where I thought we would build our lives together. I had so many plans and dreams for us; together we'd take on challenges and overcome them hand-in-hand. We'd have children and watch them grow. They'd leave and we'd grow old together. In my mind, everything was perfect, but it had all been a lie.

He'd been in the UK for a week when I told him, my eyes brimming with joyful tears, that I was pregnant. My excitement was turned to despair in an instant at his bitter reaction. He told me he had used me to get into the country, and that was all. I was nothing to him but a free pass to live here. I couldn't believe it; I was devastated. It set me on a downward spiral that quickly spun me into a pit of hopelessness.

That's when the abuse started. I was powerless to stop him, begging him not to hurt our unborn baby as he threw me around. I lived in wretched fear, losing myself a little more with each day that slipped by, becoming invisible as a dark depression seeped in to remove any happiness I once had.

He took all of my money and frittered it away on alcohol and whatever else he wanted. He left me nothing, not even to pay my bills. The landlord demanded rent and it was my sole responsibility, as the house was in my name. My husband had been threatening other tenants, staggering around in a drunken stupor and hurling insults at anyone he passed. I saw him roaming around with another woman. He'd arrive home and I would be disgusted at him and what my life had become.

He became increasingly angry and violent as I became more vulnerable. One night, he came home in a drunken rage. I was such an easy target;

his punch-bag, his stress ball. He beat me then wrapped his dirty fingers around my neck until lights flashed through my blurred vision. Then he pulled out the knife; I thought my baby and I were going to die.

By some miracle I managed to escape. To this day I don't know how, but I ran into the street without any shoes. I didn't think; I just ran for my life. People were staring at me as I ran in confusion, tears flowing down my face. I headed for the train station and looked over the bridge. I wanted to jump but a voice spoke to me; 'don't kill yourself and your baby; I still love you.' Through it all, I knew deep down that God would help me.

I headed to the police station and immediately they rushed me to A&E. They arrested my husband but he was soon released on bail. I was terrified. I found out that he told the police I had had an affair and that it wasn't his child. I couldn't believe my ears; how had he suddenly become the victim and not me? Before I could do anything more, I discovered my husband had left the country. He took all my money and left me pregnant and alone.

I was devastated. I had no one to call and no one to turn to in my hour of need. All my family were thousands of miles away in India, so when I went into labour I didn't know a single kind person to call on to take me to the hospital. I dragged myself there, fearing for my baby. The rain poured down in icy sheets and I didn't have a single penny for a taxi or a bus, so I walked with a mother's desire to protect my child. It was the only thing that kept my feet moving. I reached the maternity ward at ten at night where, finally, I could receive care. They induced full labour and my baby was born.

I couldn't believe how my life had changed so dramatically. In India, I had qualified as a biomedical scientist and worked in pathology. However, I couldn't find a paid position in the UK. Instead, I found work as a carer, but I barely had enough hours to earn anything. Sometimes, I'd be lucky to get two hours a week, which was not enough to support both my baby and me. I tried every avenue to get help; I pleaded with my family in India to spare whatever they could, but I come from a poor family with their own needs.

The Jobcentre let me apply for a crisis loan to bridge the gap, but it was only a short-term solution. I slipped further and further into depression as doors closed and hope began to fade. Meals were missed and nights were spent staring into the inky blackness of the ceiling, as sleep never outbid the fearful thoughts. I was desperate to give my baby a better life, but the future felt so bleak. I just couldn't see a way out.

Then, when I was clinging to the end of the rope; when I was about to fall beyond saving; my social worker recommended Christians Against Poverty.

'They'll never be able to help me,' I remember stating, bluntly, 'I'm too far gone'.

I mustered the courage to give it one last go. I picked up the phone, dialed the number and took my first step on a path to freedom.

When Nikki, the Debt Coach, came to my house, I wasn't really expecting much. I thought I might get some financial advice, but ultimately be told there was nothing that could be done. Up until now everything had felt hopeless and I didn't see how this lady could help me. Instead, I was told that everything was going to be okay. CAP could help.

'How can CAP do it?' I asked, struggling to believe I could be helped, 'How can they turn this mountain into a mustard seed?'

Every question I had was answered with compassion. Every doubt I presented was greeted with reassurance. Nikki was so loving and genuine that I felt I could trust her. She collected all the paperwork that had been gathering: the final demands, bills and threats of further action. She put it all in an envelope and told me CAP were going to take care of it. It all seemed so easy and I struggled to believe it was possible.

The pressure from debt collectors stopped and I knew the staff at CAP were working on my behalf to negotiate settlements and better repayments. A budget was put together for me; one that would allow me to feed my baby and myself and still pay what I owed. It wasn't easy, but it felt like I had been guided onto the right track. I could finally get a foothold and start climbing out of the hole of depression.

There were times when I wanted to give up, like when a bailiff arrived, announcing a huge debt that I hadn't known about. Just when things felt like they were getting better, I would be thrown back into despair. The only thing that kept me going was CAP. They'd always keep in touch with me, making sure that I was coping. They listened with genuine care and that helped ease the sting of my situation.

Not long after I started working with CAP, I was invited to go on a Discovery Break: a short holiday for CAP clients to have a break away from everything. In my state, I couldn't understand why Nikki insisted that I go. Perhaps she knew that I was close to the end. I tried to make excuses as to why I couldn't go, but she made sure that everything was taken care of. I was worried about how I would get there with the baby. I had no money and no transport. However, CAP organised all of my travel to make sure I could go. They thought of everything and nothing was too much trouble. I'm so glad I went.

In just four short days, my life was completely transformed. From the minute I arrived, I was treated with so much love and care by the CAP staff; they were like angels. They even thought of the little things and I was overwhelmed by their kindness. Ever since my husband had left, I had to do everything for my baby and I. I had forgotten what it was like to let someone else look after me for a change. I didn't realise how exhausted and stressed I was. CAP took care of everything, and slowly I allowed myself to relax. Every morning I would wake up feeling lighter. For once, I wasn't worried, I had lot of wonderful food and my baby wasn't crying. Before, I never had time to do what I wanted, but here I could be myself.

One evening that I will never forget was a pamper night. They treated everyone to foot massages, manicures and facials. I was so surprised to find out that all the people providing the treatments were actually volunteers. I just couldn't believe how much they wanted to give me. The whole time I was treated like royalty and I lacked nothing. I felt like it was a little taste of heaven. I was smiling without realising it and my heart, which had been shattered for so long, was mended. I was in my Father's house and I had nothing to fear. For the first time the cloud over me lifted and the Holy Spirit filled me. I no longer thought about myself but wanted to help others and offered to give people massages.

By the end of the break, I didn't want to leave. I had made so many new friends and I just wanted to give back to everyone who had helped me. It was a fantastic few days and I left that break feeling utterly revived. It strengthened me physically, mentally and spiritually.

My journey has been a long and tough one. However, last year I went through bankruptcy and now I am totally free, happy and in control of my finances. I have always been a Catholic and I know now that it was God who brought me through the darkest times. I can look back now and see how he led me to CAP and that saved my life. On the break, I was reminded of my faith in him and his love for me as he lifted the dark cloud from my life and replaced it with his Holy Spirit. He opened my eyes to a new perspective on life and I can see that, through my struggles, he is always with me. I feel that I now have a fresh start with my daughter, away from the hurt and abuse. Finally, we can put the past behind us and focus on the future God has for us instead.

Restored

Mervyn McWatters

It's 3am. I can't sleep, as usual. The same thought keeps spiralling around my head: 'What if I never get out of debt?' I have already lost my job, my car and my house; I just can't see an end to it all. I climb out of bed and wander into the living room of my small flat. It's winter and I can see my breath in the damp air. I shiver and pull my dressing gown tighter around the layers of clothes underneath. I am wearing most of the clothes I own, but it doesn't seem to make a difference. It has been another day of deciding between buying food and heating the house. Today, hunger won.

I pace the floor of my flat and think over my options. I have tried absolutely everything, but it seems the harder I try, the worse it gets. I am out of ideas. A familiar voice speaks softly, almost like a thought drifting through my mind, *Just give up. What's the point? Might as well just end it all now, it's the only option.'* I try to shrug it off, 'Maybe I will get an interview tomorrow, maybe that will be the one?' A sinking feeling drops down to the pit of my stomach. 'Who am I kidding? Even if I got a job tomorrow, it would take me everything I earn, and more, to get out of this debt.'

I wander out onto my balcony and peer through the night sky across the little rows of houses where everyone else is sound asleep. If only there was someone I could talk to. I feel like the only person in the world right now. I have my son, but it's not fair to put this pressure on him. Time is dragging, an hour has barely passed but it feels like a lifetime. I can't seem to shake this sick feeling of hopelessness.

My heart is pumping fast. My emotions are all over the place. I place my hands on the cold balcony railing and squeeze it tight as a voice whispers again, *'It's okay Mervyn, you have done your best. There is no way out. It's best just to jump and end it all.'* The voice is convincing and I entertain the idea as I look over the railing. I'm on the ninth floor; there would be no coming back.

'But what about my son? I can't do this to him,' I tell the voice. *'Your son and family will understand. Go on, just jump and all your problems will be over,'* says the voice, reassuringly. 'I guess so, it's not like I haven't tried really hard to get a job,' I say. 'And it's not my fault that I am up against lots of applicants much younger than me. Perhaps my family would be better off without me?' I close my eyes and imagine it all ending.

Just then, another voice interrupts. This voice is different to the one before, **'Mervyn don't throw your life away, you are important to me,'** it says. I open my eyes and hold my breath as I listen again, **'You are loved by so many and I love you too. I will help you get through this ... I am with you ... trust me.'**

'Trust me, trust me,' the voice gently repeats.

'Okay,' I reply.

* * *

The voice that cut through my despair was God's and I am so thankful to him for speaking to me in what was one of the darkest times of my life. Everyone has a breaking point that can lead to a mental breakdown or worse and, like so many others, that breaking point for me was debt.

It all started when I lost my job in June 2009. I worked for a family business, selling advertising space for a business magazine. It was a well-paid job and I was really good at it. I had a comfortable life. I drove a nice car. I had savings, enough money to pay all the bills and go on nice holidays. I was really happy; I never dreamt that I could end up in debt. I had worked my whole life and I was confident, even when I lost my job, that I would find employment again. It just never occurred to me that four years on I would still be looking for permanent work.

That year was a tough time for the economy. The recession hit everyone hard - nobody knew when it would be over. There was uncertainty all around and a lot of people lost their jobs in order for businesses to stay afloat. Because I worked in advertising, I became one of those people – it was one of the first areas where cut backs were made. Looking back, I suppose it was obvious but at the time I really didn't expect it. I guess I assumed that because I was good at my job and I got on well with the team, my position in the company was safe. So when my boss came in to see me one day, I wasn't prepared at all.

The look on his face immediately told me that something was wrong. He had a real sadness in his eyes as he told me he was sorry but he had no other choice but to let me go. I knew that it was something he hadn't considered lightly but it was still a real blow, as I hadn't seen it coming. I told him I understood and left feeling relatively positive that I could find something new.

Being the character that I am, I believed I would be back in employment within three to four months at the most. I left work with the confidence and faith that it was simply a bump in the road and in no time at all, I would be back in work. However, the weeks slowly turned into months and I started to lose count of the job applications I had made. I had several interviews, but nothing came of them. It was hard to take the repeated knock backs but, still convinced that something would come along soon, I ploughed on. In the meantime, I used my savings to keep up with the mortgage and bills. I had plenty of savings, so at first I wasn't too worried, but it was surprising how quickly they diminished.

I began to feel pangs of desperation as I applied for anything and everything. I was worried because I knew my skills didn't match the job specifications, but time was ticking by and I knew I couldn't be picky. Determined to carry on, I churned out application after application but my confidence slowly eroded as the rejection letters trickled in. 'We have decided to hire someone whose background and experience more closely match our need,' they said. 'We appreciate your interest in this position and wish you every success in your job search.' My heart sank as I realised that the situation was tough for everyone and there must be hundreds of people like me applying for jobs. The problem was, I was up against applicants half my age and I didn't have a specific trade, I was a sales person applying for jobs I didn't have experience in. I was fighting a losing battle.

The savings pot soon began to run dry and eventually I was left with nothing. Panic hit me as I remembered the property I had in Turkey. I had bought it as an investment for my pension on top of my current mortgage and, whilst I was working, it hadn't been a problem keeping up with the repayments. Now I had no income and no savings and I wondered how on earth would I manage. I felt sick. I grabbed the phone and called the mortgage company. Explaining my situation, I felt some relief as they agreed to put me on an 'interest only' repayment. At least that would buy me some time until I could think of a more permanent solution.

With no money at all, I headed to the Jobcentre to sign on for Job Seeker's Allowance. I felt numb as I walked up the steps. How had this happened? I had worked all my life; I was a confident guy with lots of potential. I had never had to 'sign on'. I desperately hoped I would wake up soon and realise it was all a bad dream. But I didn't and, instead, things just continued to get worse.

The mortgage company kept calling me to check if my situation had changed. They were keen to know when I would be able to make a contribution. Months had passed and all I had to live off was my Job Seeker's Allowance. I simply had nothing to give them. I dreaded each call and my response was always the same, 'No, things are still the same; I am still searching for work but hopefully I will get something soon.' The words sounded positive as they came out of my mouth, but inside my hope of finding work was dwindling.

Soon the calls turned to threats and they told me that if I didn't make a contribution they would take me to court. 'Surely it won't come to that? Surely something will change?' I would try to convince myself. But my fears were realised when a letter landed on my doormat. It was from a solicitor telling me that they would take me to court for bankruptcy if I didn't pay something in a month. My stomach churned. It had been almost nine months and no matter how much I had wanted to, I just hadn't been able to pay anything to them. I sank onto the floor and stared at the piece of paper in shock.

I felt the panic rise up through my body as thoughts rushed through my mind, 'What would I do if I lost the house? Where would I go?' I'd never been in that situation before; not knowing what the future held. It was terrifying. At night, I would lie awake going over and over in my mind what would happen to me. I took the letter to the Housing Executive for some advice, but they told me that because I was single and not married with young children, by law I wasn't 'a priority' for housing. I felt dread creep over me as they told me it would be at least nine to twelve months until I got something! In the meantime, they could put me in a shared hostel. I was horrified. The prospect of sharing a large room with drug addicts and alcoholics for a year was terrifying. I asked if there was an alternative and they said that if I went and found a private landlord myself who was willing to take me on, then they would provide me with housing benefits.

I wasted no time in my search for a house. I was excited when I discovered an advert for a large house that let out rooms and immediately booked an appointment to view it. When I went to visit they said they only had one room left, so I rushed in an application. I was overjoyed when they called to tell me I could have it. I couldn't believe something was finally going right for once. I have been there ever since; praise God ,his hand was on it! It was a real relief as it wasn't long before the dreaded day arrived when my house was repossessed. I held onto my car for as long as possible so I could go to interviews, but eventually I had to give that up too. It was like everything was being taken from me and I found it hard to stay positive. I felt like I was just trying to survive, fighting the depression. Each day, I would drag myself to the local library and trawl the job sites but it was incredibly hard to stay positive and motivated.

If that wasn't enough, over Easter my older brother, David, died. He lived in Perth, Australia and under normal circumstances I would have booked a flight to go there for his funeral. However, I had no savings, no job and my only income was my unemployment benefit. It was impossible for me to go and that weighed very heavily on my heart.

One day, I was chatting to my advisor at the Jobcentre. He must have seen how bad things were by the look of hopelessness on my face and he pointed me to a poster on the wall, which read, 'Struggling with debt?' He explained that someone had recently come to visit from a charity called Christians Against Poverty, which helps people get out of debt. He said there was a local debt centre in Belfast and, handing me a leaflet, he suggested I give them a call. A glimmer of hope crept into my mind at the idea of someone who could help me, but still I was sceptical. My situation felt beyond help, so I stuffed the leaflet in my pocket and headed home. It took me forty-eight hours to muster up the courage to call CAP. Although it was a freephone number, my shame and embarrassment held me back from making the call. I wasn't sure what to say or how they would react when I told them how bad it was. I was worried that people would think it was my fault that I was in debt.

To my relief, they didn't judge me at all. Within one hour of calling up their head office, the manager of the local CAP Debt Centre in Belfast, Brian, called me back to set up an appointment to come and visit me. That was the start of my recovery. I had tried everything in my own strength, but it was useless. I finally realised that the situation wasn't my fault and that I needed help. Brian gathered all of my paperwork and sent it away to CAP's head office. They worked out my income and outgoings and told me if I got any more threatening letters or calls, to tell them to contact CAP. It was such a fantastic feeling to know someone was taking the burden off me.

Brian was amazing; he is still one of the best guys in my life. He is so genuine and down to earth and he is constantly smiling - I think he must even smile in his sleep! Another man who played a big part in my journey with CAP is Gerry. He is a CAP Befriender, or as I call him, 'Brian's right hand man'. Gerry took me under his wing whilst Brian was visiting other clients. We would meet up regularly in the shopping centre, he'd take me for a coffee and we would chat. His support and encouragement would boost my morale and keep me going. We are still very good friends.

Gerry also brought me hampers from the local church where Brian's CAP Debt Centre is based. They had things like cornflakes, tins of beans, toothpaste and washing up liquid in them – the basics I needed but didn't have. Before CAP, some weeks I only had two days' worth of food, as I couldn't afford both food and heating. The hampers were such a great blessing and I am truly thankful even now to all the members of Carnmoney Presbyterian Church, who faithfully donate food and other items every Sunday to go into these hampers. They made a huge difference to me and I know they will for so many other people who are now in desperate situations like I was.

Brian passed on my details to CAP's head office in Bradford and I was assigned caseworkers to manage my debts and negotiate with creditors on my behalf. Ali was my first caseworker there. She was a lovely girl, very supportive and would regularly ring and email me to see how I was. One time, she even sent me a little book of prayer as an encouragement. I also worked with another guy called Matt. He was really nice; we were like a big brother and a little brother. Brian, Gerry, Ali and Matt together were like my second family. They are special to me and always will be.

I started to feel better once my debts were being dealt with, but the property in Turkey still hung over me like a dark cloud. I had put it on the market, but it wouldn't sell. In the meantime the team at CAP tried really hard to have my debts cleared through insolvency, as I had no income to pay off my debts. However, the Official Receiver wouldn't entertain it until the overseas property had sold. It felt like a real battle and I wondered if it would ever end. However, after some time, against all odds, CAP managed to agree closure. Whilst I lost that property, I am happy to report that on 4 October 2012, at the Royal Courts of Justice in Belfast, I became debt free. We all cheered as we left court.

What does being debt free mean to me? It means I have peace of mind (and a good night's sleep). My self-respect and self-esteem have returned.

The burden of stress has gone. It means I have my life back and I can now look forward to happy days again. Debt makes you feel like you are being tortured, exposed and judged. When you feel that kind of pressure it's hard to stay positive. When I realised I could no longer solve my debt problems through my own efforts, the light of hope went out of my life and stress entered into it. Stress grows until you get to a position of despair; you feel trapped, a slave to debt. But CAP changed my life. They stood by me all the way and kept me afloat.

As a Christian, I have questioned God, 'Why have you allowed me to go through this? I lost everything'. But looking back, it's amazing to see the way God works and I know his timing is perfect. As I was coming out of debt, I discovered that he was using my experience to help others. I shared my story once and afterwards a girl gave her heart to God and joined CAP to get help with her debts. All glory to him! Unless you have been through it, you can't speak to anyone about it. If you had looked at my background, salary and lifestyle you would never have said I would be in debt. However, there are no guarantees in life and everyone is capable of falling into debt. When you go out and about in your community, you may pass hundreds of people and many will be in debt, but you couldn't stop and pick them out. Everyone wears a mask and it isn't until you get home behind closed doors that you take it off. I wore that mask; I know what it was like.

But that's not the end of my story. Although debt free, I was still unemployed and living on a very tight budget. I was keen to find work again, but my confidence had really taken a knock, as it had been three years since I had last worked. When I heard that my church had launched a CAP Job Club to help people find employment again, I decided to join. The club involved an eight-week course that covered lots of practical advice, such as CV writing and interviewing techniques. It also had individual and group support to encourage people who, like me, had been out of work for a long time and were feeling particularly discouraged. A lovely couple called Sharon and Clarke ran the club; they were so friendly and open that you could feel the warmth as you walked in. For some people it was the first time they had stepped into a church hall in their lives, but it wasn't a problem and they felt very welcomed. Each time I would come away feeling inspired, encouraged and motivated. I would recommend it to anyone!

One day, I got the call that I had been looking forward to for such a long time. I was sat in my local library as normal, checking my email, when my mobile rang. I headed outside and answered the call to discover it was a person from one of the job agencies that I had registered with. 'Mervyn, we would like to offer you a job,' said the person on the other end. I stood still in complete disbelief to what I was hearing. 'You start in one week's time.' It took a few minutes to sink in but as I headed back indoors, I felt the biggest smile creep across my face. I sat back down, my face beaming like the cat that got the cream! I remembered how, when I became debt free, I had thought, 'Can it ever get better than this?' Well, that day it did.

My journey started in 2009, unemployed, which lead to debt. Praise God, after four years my journey finished on a high; being debt free and starting life again with a job! Fantastic. All glory to our beautiful God. CAP is a fantastic organisation, blessed and ordained by God. I know in my heart that everyone there is singing from the same song sheet and each and every one plays an important part. By bringing me to CAP, God has created so much goodness from my journey! I thank CAP for all they have done. I also wish to thank my son, my family and my friends, who have supported me through the last four years. Finally, my hope and prayers are for the people who are in debt, that they too will take the golden opportunity of asking CAP for help. And when each person becomes debt free, that they also will receive the happiness again that they once had, just as I have.

A new beginning.

Ray and Patti Penn

Flicking through wedding magazines, I couldn't believe how we'd ever be able to do it. You always hear about weddings costing thousands of pounds. Well, in our position that just wasn't possible. Debts are a drain on your dreams as well as your pockets. So it was back to treading water. The little left after living goes on debts and we go nowhere.

Then there is the constant ringing of the telephone, I mean consistently ringing – thirty, forty times per day. I hated that phone, but we couldn't unplug it, it might be the hospital – knots in your stomach every time you answer it. Having to stay home to care for Patti wasn't the best situation to start with, but add in the phone calls and the pressure really mounts. Her health is one of the reasons we were struggling with debt and the stress made her condition a lot worse. She needed a full time carer, so there was no chance of me working, and a carer's living allowance doesn't allow for much, especially once the credit mounts up.

As for me, I used to be a teacher and lecturer. Along with some of the other things I used to do, I was quite well paid. So I got used to the lifestyle and the income in the bank. Credit cards were the norm, but the money was there to back it up. When my health unexpectedly deteriorated, I had to leave work and the cards continued to plug the gap. The problem was that the money wasn't in the bank anymore. Then when Patti needed me to be her full time carer, there was no going back to work. No work, no boost in income, no possibility of paying off debts. You think that it is down to you to sort it, so you try to balance things, scrimp, move stuff around, but it never works.

Before I met Patti, she was in a difficult relationship. Her partner used to abuse her. Add to that her health problems – she has suffered with a neurological condition that is similar to Parkinson's Disease for twenty years, as well as back problems and needing a gastric bypass – it wasn't an easy life. What with her relationship breakdown and only benefits to live on, simply trying to live became a struggle for her. Patti was really keen to go back to her job as a nurse. However, her health problems meant work was not an option. When she was told she couldn't work it was a real blow for her.

We had heard about CAP a while ago when we were having a BBQ with friends. A lady we knew, called Julie, was there and she mentioned she was working for a debt counselling charity called CAP. We wondered who CAP were but didn't think much more. Patti had been with a debt company and had been faithfully paying in, but seven years in, she was no better off and they just said, we can't help you anymore and dropped her! It was devastating, as she had been working so hard.

It wasn't until things got really bad that we remembered CAP. I was already struggling to deal with Patti's deteriorating health when I found out my daughter was in an abusive relationship and had fallen pregnant. The stress of trying to help her and Patti, and manage a lot of other things caused me to have a nervous breakdown. I went for counselling and it took a while for things to settle down, but then after Christmas we took in our four-week-old grandson to care for full time. It was yet another strain on our already fragile finances.

We were desperately trying to pay off debts and would just begin building a relationship with one company when we would get a letter telling us a debt collection company had bought our debts from them. It felt like the goal posts kept moving and the amount we owed never seemed to reduce. In fact, one time we went overdrawn and this caused a chain reaction of interest and charges. We couldn't pay them off so they spiralled and compounded. That month we had £750 of bank charges. Everything went pear shaped very quickly, and eventually we ended up with £42,000 of debt. When I had another breakdown, we realised we couldn't carry on like we were.

That was the point we contacted Julie. Within days, she came around and told us what CAP could offer if we booked an appointment with them. Before we officially started working with CAP, I had a third breakdown. It was a very stressful time and the debt just further compounded everything. Looking back I don't know what we would have done if CAP hadn't stepped in.

We couldn't believe the service was free but we were both still sceptical because of the previous organisation Patti had been with. But when Julie came to visit us in our home, we could tell that CAP weren't like the other companies we had dealt with. Julie was interested in us. Actually interested in us. After watching the CAP DVD, we had a good look through the pack and decided that was the way to go. It was fairly obvious early on; one of us would have to go bankrupt.

We grabbed three or four carrier bags of unopened envelopes and Julie sat with us and trawled through them all. We had had this huge pile which had just got bigger and bigger. We knew it was there but we hadn't dared to open it. Just to lose that pile of letters was so liberating! It must have taken all afternoon to sort all the letters. Julie filled up a huge envelope with them and told us it would all go off to CAP's head office. That felt really good – we knew we couldn't face the content of the letters ourselves and we felt we could trust CAP to do it for us. Knowing they would contact all the different creditors really took the pressure off.

From then on everything happened really quickly. Within what seemed like days, we got a budget and we knew how much we would have to pay and who our primary creditors were. Although the phone calls kept coming, being able to tell them that they would have to speak to our representatives at CAP felt great. Soon the number of calls dropped as CAP got in touch with each creditor. I felt like I finally had a little bit of protection against these huge organisations that were demanding money from me. I felt like David, from the Bible, who was up against the giant Goliath and CAP was my catapult.

We even got to go on a short holiday with CAP, one of their Discovery Breaks. It was amazing to have that break; we really needed it. We had been caring for our grandson full time for eleven months and it was our first weekend off. We knew nothing about it other than everything was paid for and we just had to turn up. The staff couldn't do enough for us; they were all so friendly. Each day, there were sessions that we could choose to go to on topics like anger and forgiveness. They were things I was facing due to the pressure we were under and past issues with my family. I'd been to counselling at home, but I found the forgiveness session very powerful.

It was the first time I realised that to forgive someone didn't mean I actually had to see them face-to-face, but I could do it from afar. I had never tried to forgive them because the thought of facing them was too much. The session made a huge difference and, with God's strength, I was able to forgive those people there and then for all the hurt they had caused me. By my next counselling appointment, just a few days after the session, I realised the majority of my hurt and lack of trusting people close to me had gone.

Imagine that; eighteen months of counselling couldn't do what this one-hour session on forgiveness did. Since then, I have been able to meet with the people who I had forgiven, one of whom I hadn't spoken to in a long time. Sadly, after four months of us getting in contact again he passed away. It really made me stop and think about the bigger picture – it is like God knew his time was limited and so he helped me reconcile things before it was too late.

They really were amazing people that we met on this break. It was so nice to be able to put the past behind us and move on. Just one more step on the road to us being able to get married and start a future together.

Since first getting in touch with CAP, life hasn't always been easy, but the great thing is that we knew we were on our way out of our problems. It was a great feeling the day CAP told me I had become debt free. I am so grateful to everyone who worked hard to help me and get my Debt Relief Order sorted.

Once we got to a stage where our debts were dealt with enough, we felt we were free to finally get married. We really couldn't start our new life together with them hanging over our heads. By working with CAP, we had been able to build up some modest savings while living to the budget they created for us. This meant we could have a small family wedding with some simple pleasures – cups of tea and takeaway pizza.

Patti's wedding dress was a gift from her cousin, which was amazing. She looked beautiful in it. I made the kilt for my outfit. We had the reception at the former Teesside Rowing Club; it was a glorious day and we got to enjoy the weather. We even got a wedding discount on the takeaway pizza.

Some time after the wedding, we just had to visit those who had made it possible, so we called CAP's head office up to arrange a visit. We had some wedding favours that we wanted to give to all of their staff for what they had done for us. We drove to Bradford. Patti had her wedding dress on and I was in my wedding outfit. An hour or so later, we arrived at CAP and were blown away. All the staff members were waiting to greet us – cheering and celebrating. Some even had confetti.

We got to hand out the wedding favours – little packs of Love Hearts sweets – to all of them and say thank you for all they had done. It meant so much to be able to thank them in person and I could see that they were excited to see us. Everyone seemed genuinely pleased that they had helped us. That's the difference; we were people to them, not just a number on a system. We had some photos taken with the whole staff and then some great pictures in the sunshine outside the office with them throwing confetti.

Since visiting CAP, Patti got the call to say she is also debt free. It is such a great feeling to have come out the other side – a brilliant start to our married life together. It's been a long road and certainly not easy, but we are married and now both of us are debt free. We have space to breathe and a new start. I can enjoy life now and I'm looking forward to my future with my wife.

Patti

Whenever Ray calls me his wife I go all squidgy inside. Every time someone calls me Mrs, or I tell them I'm married, something inside me wants to dance, sing and shine. It makes me giggle; I'm like a young girl who has met her prince charming. It's so lovely being married to Ray and it was CAP who made that possible.

The very least we could do was pay them a visit to say thank you. We would have had each member of staff at the wedding if we could have. Instead, we made a trip to CAP's head office and brought everyone a little part of the day – wedding favours; small packs of love hearts – my favourite sweets.

When we arrived at Jubilee Mill, I was completely overwhelmed! I had only really expected a couple of folk to be there and so was utterly blown away as I stepped out of the car. We were greeted by two hundred CAP staff cheering and clapping us. It was absolutely awesome, really wonderful. We told the staff a little about our day and thanked them all because it was them who gave us the freedom to get married.

The day itself couldn't have been better; the sun shone and it was gloriously warm. I had been worried about being outside, because with my health problems, my body shuts down if it gets cold. But we were blessed with great weather and everything went without a hitch. Being on a really tight budget didn't matter, because I had all the people who meant the most there with me.

It would have been easy to go to town and go overboard on spending, but for me it wasn't about the event. Yes, I wanted it to be nice and something to look back on with real pleasure, but it was ultimately about marrying the man I love. People were incredibly generous and showered us with gifts, like my wedding dress – I am so thankful for all of them.

It's amazing to think where I am now compared to where I was several years back, before I even met Ray. I was stuck in a controlling and violent relationship, which led me into debt. My previous partner would force me to sign documents for loans, credit cards and all sorts of things, and then run them up to the max. My health had already begun to deteriorate at this point. The medication I was on made me confused and often sapped any strength I had to challenge him. The times I did, his response was one of violence. He would hit me or put a knife at my throat until I submitted. Those times, I was under no illusions what the punishment would be for my son or myself.

I knew we had to get out and, somehow, I managed to summon enough physical and mental strength to leave. After hours in court and with the solicitors, I had an injunction granted and the police moved my ex-partner out of our house. Finally I was free, or so I thought. Whilst my ex-partner wasn't allowed within a certain distance of me, he took that literally, standing on the edge to watch and intimidate me. I was terrified; wherever I went, he would follow and would always be watching. Also, it wasn't long before I was sucked into the trap of debt that I was left with. I felt no freer than when I was living with him.

Moving house helped and slowly I began to feel less afraid. It wasn't until I was with Ray that I really stopped looking over my shoulder or out the door before I left. We first met when he came over to fix my computer, someone recommended him as an IT whiz. He came around and we just clicked; there was something about him. We knew there was a real spark between us – it quickly turned into a wonderful relationship.

For a while, all was going well and we were doing okay financially. Ray was working and I was paying back my debts through a debt management company. Then after a few years, my health took a real turn for the worse. Ray had to give up his job to look after me. My health had been up and down for years, ever since I first fell ill and was given just a week to live. I remember it well because I had just been offered two fantastic nursing positions in local hospices, but just before I was due to start work I was rushed into hospital. Somehow I pulled through, but when I finally came out of hospital I couldn't feed or dress myself. An assortment of carers, family and friends rallied around to help me, but without a diagnosis they struggled to give me the right medication.

Over the years it has been like a merry-go-round: going in and out of hospital, having lots of tests and seeing so many consultants. I had an array of different medications that sometimes made me better, and sometimes made me worse. More than once, I nearly died. For a long time, no one could figure out what was wrong with me, until I saw a specialist in London who finally gave me a diagnosis. I was relieved to have some answers, but was devastated to know that my condition would only get worse. Any hope I had of going back to work was crushed.

When Ray had to give up his work because of me, I felt dreadful. With bills to pay and two teenagers to look after, it was incredibly tough. People say babies are expensive but I think teenagers are worse! The council had a disabled access extension built onto our little house, but then we had to furnish it and that didn't come easy or cheap. Things continued to be up and down and the kids had their own issues. Putting two families together is never an easy thing to do and, on top of all that, Ray had his own health issues. Life just wasn't easy and throughout it all our debts never went away. One day, out of the blue, the debt management company I was working with dropped a bomb on me.

'We're sorry but we just can't help you anymore,' they said.

Seven years of regularly paying in at least £400 a month and that was it – no further explanation. I was in despair. I just don't know what we would have done if we hadn't found out about CAP. At first, I felt so embarrassed because I already knew Julie personally. The idea that she would come into our house and find out what a mess we had made was mortifying. I was ashamed to share that with anyone, let alone a friend.

We had piles of envelopes all around so we gathered together as many of them as we could. We must have handed over wads and wads of paper, and each time I winced with shame. 'That's fine,' she would reply to me with each handful, 'I will sort it out, don't worry'. I apologised over and over again, but still she wasn't fazed. 'Don't be daft, I have seen far worse!' she said reassuringly, as she headed out the door. I sat and wept with relief.

When the budget came back, it was much easier than we had expected – CAP gave us so much more leeway than we'd had before. For the first time, we had enough money for food and we set aside money for the kids. All that and they never charged us a penny! It was amazing to be able to tell creditors to contact CAP, and not have to deal with the letters; just simply put them in an envelope to CAP. Slowly the stress eased and, as we relaxed, our relationship improved.

When I look back on when we were in the thick of things, I see the stress we were under as a couple. Debt was merely the tip of the iceberg of things going on, but it nearly finished us. My health needs were forever mounting and Ray felt an incredible weight of pressure to be in control of everything. But he couldn't, it was too much for anyone to deal with everything we were facing. To know Ray now you wouldn't have guessed he used to get so angry. He was so upset, tired and frustrated. It's no wonder he had a few breakdowns in one year. We had some awful rows and both of us had patches where we were really low. Just one last attempt to talk – that was what kept us together – one last attempt to fight through it. And I am so glad we did.

The CAP holiday was a really significant time for us as a couple. It was the first time we had been away, just the two of us. Being a private person, I was worried how Ray would respond to all the other people and the activities, but he really surprised me. 'We might as well join in with everything,' he said. And we did. Ray went on the forgiveness session and found it life changing. He really is a different person – I can see how he has let go of the past. For me, the session on worry was a real eye opener. I had always been a real worrywart. The session helped me put things into perspective and decide what wasn't worth hanging on to. We made a list of worries and binned the ones we needed to let go of – I threw my whole list in! It was very freeing.

Now, we are both debt free and it's taken less than two years! To think before I was paying a massive amount of money every month for nothing, but CAP sorted everything out so quickly. Their budget meant I paid in a lot less every month and I knew it was all going to pay my bills and clear my debts. Being debt free has made a huge difference to our relationship. The stress eased and because of the way CAP worked, we had savings for the first time in nine and a half years. It wasn't a massive amount, but it was enough for us to finally be able to get married and that was wonderful! The whole process with CAP has meant a lot to us and although we still live on a tight budget, we are keen to give something back. We think that giving just a couple of pounds a month to help another family who are still in debt is worth it.

I continue to struggle with my health; my neck and back are effectively crumbling, so I am in constant pain. The amount of morphine just to help me stand up is enough to kill a horse, but not my pain. Sometimes I deal with it and sometimes I despair. In those moments I just have to sit still, be quiet and just know God's there. It is hard and sometimes it doesn't feel like God is close, however, I know he never leaves me and I am confident of his love for me. Whilst it is hard to understand the reason for all this pain, I trust my life is part of his master plan. What I do know is that Ray is part of the plan and I am excited about our future married life together.

Rescued

Sarah Jane Hawthorne

All parents go through days when they long for a bit of peace and can take a little break. I remember what it was like without the kids running around and screaming for attention; when I could sit down for five minutes and take a breather from the endless onslaught and responsibility. Children are such a blessing, but sometimes it all just gets too much.

A mother who loves her children will protect them at all costs, and I utterly adore mine. It is so shocking, therefore, that there came a day when I woke up and felt absolutely nothing. Parents will understand that, to get to the stage where you walk out on your children, there must be something seriously wrong with you psychologically. That's where I was; when I couldn't hold back the pressure anymore. When the weight of a life spiralling out of control eventually got too much to bear, I walked out of my house and into a mental abyss. I was ready to leave my life, and the life of my children, behind.

That is what relentless debt does to a person, but I never thought it would happen to me. The problems started when I tried to find a purpose in my life. I needed to feel some sort of validation. I'd look for love in all the wrong places and end up getting involved with different men. I'd have fun flings with guys that gave me something to live for. They each came and went, taking a little piece of me with them when they left. I immersed myself in a culture that I thought was the high life. I'd fill my body with drugs at parties that went on until the sun came up. I knew it wasn't a healthy lifestyle then, but I was so desperate to convince myself I had everything to live for. Drugs convinced me I had lots of friends, that my life was good and that I could get a man if I wanted to. It was in these moments, when the music pounded in my ears and alcohol coursed through my body, that I would lower my inhibitions. I wasn't careful; I was desperate to feel alive. I had five children from four different men that either wanted nothing to do with their child or were a danger to be around.

I knew it was time to put the parties behind me and decided that I would build my life around my children. My amazing kids always held me together when I was falling apart, and I put everything into being the best mum I could be.

Then the debt started. It was only a little at first; I just spent a little extra here and there to buy nice treats for the kids. When I was out shopping, I'd buy them presents with store cards and credit cards. As a single mum of five with low self-esteem, I was still desperate for the approval of those around me. I wanted my kids to look immaculate and have all the latest toys and gadgets so that the other mums at the school gate would look in awe at how well I was doing.

'Five children! And without a man!' I imagined them saying, talking amongst themselves and wondering what my secret was. I relished in their impressed looks and admiring comments; of course, the secret of my apparent success was a fake one.

I wasn't coping. I didn't have the money to support such a lavish lifestyle and borrowing had become so easy. My teenage son, Joel, cashed in on my generosity and I found it increasingly hard to say no to his demands. Joel was going through such a difficult phase of life and needed a firmer hand. I knew I should have put my foot down, established boundaries and taken responsibility. I couldn't break the cycle, and Joel in particular knew he could ask for anything and I would alway say yes, without fail.

The debts began to rise as my credit rating plummeted. I had to take out more loans, but very quickly, companies realised that they'd never see the money again and stopped lending to me. Still I needed more cash and I didn't care where it came from. I resorted to borrowing from people who didn't ask questions and didn't need details. They didn't care that my credit rating was in a shambles; they didn't even check. I was desperate. It seemed so easy at the time; cash in hand, no questions asked, paid back with interest dumped on top.

It was the worst decision I could have made, but it was the only option I had. I didn't worry about the consequences. I can look back now and realise that it should never have been an option, but at the time, it didn't matter about the future. I could only think about getting more money to feed the life I was trying to fake. I quickly fell behind on the repayments, the stress increased and my life became a living nightmare. I was hounded for money on a daily basis as the interest compounded and increased. Stress turned to worry, and worry turned to fear. Like a swelling inside, it built up until it consumed every moment of my life. It got so much that I had a miscarriage.

I reached my breaking point two years after my youngest son was born. The fear had led to illness and I couldn't cope anymore. My body was shutting down emotionally and I began to build up walls to protect myself. I shut everyone out and retreated into despair. I'd been carrying the weight of responsibility for so long and it had become too much. There was nothing left to hope for and no end in sight. Each day, I simply stumbled through life, trying to hide my anxiety from the kids whilst wondering how I was going to feed them. Getting food on the table was momentary relief, before the reality of my situation would take over again. I was so emotional and on edge that I didn't know what to do; I simply wasn't myself. I tried to cover the pain of my miscarriage and the depression from debt with a fake smile, but the mask was cracking.

I sent a text to my mum and sister to say they needed to look after the children. Then I walked to the harbour. I had nothing left to give, no emotion left to release. I reached the shoreline and kept walking. The sea was cold around my knees, but I kept putting one foot in front of the other; each icy step was one closer to the end. I was up to my waist when I heard the voice. It broke through the dark cloud that had consumed me like a beam of light slicing through darkness. I knew it was the voice of God.

'What on Earth do you think you're doing, Sarah?'

I stopped suddenly at the harshness of the words. If he had been any softer I wouldn't have listened; but I needed a kick up the backside. He picked me up by the scruff of the neck and reminded me that he had blessed me with five healthy kids.

'Get yourself out of the water and go back home and look after them,' he instructed, 'everything is going to be okay.'

The instruction was firm, but I knew without doubt that God was with me. I immediately turned around, walked out of the sea, and didn't look back. Now I can see that he had been trying to break into my situation for a very long time; I just hadn't allowed him in. It took me getting right to the edge of desperation to feel his love in my life and to realise that I wasn't alone. He took me by the hand and led me out of the water, and I haven't been alone since.

Since that day, I was determined to get back on track. I knew that it was time to stop trying to do it on my own and admit I needed help. My health visitor mentioned a debt counselling charity called Christians Against Poverty. With determination to climb out of the pit of debt,

I rang Jacqui, the local CAP Debt Centre Manager and poured out my situation over the phone. Her kindness and patience as I opened my heart was incredible. She put me at ease and gave me hope as she explained how CAP worked. She promised that, as soon as she could, she would make an appointment to come to my house and see me.

I found I could chat to her so easily, even in that first phone call. We talked about my situation and how I'd gotten into it. I told her about so much more than my debt and she comforted me through it all. I had never met this lady at the time, but I will never forget the genuine compassion that she gave to me, a complete stranger, on that day. We talked about God and she told me what I already knew; I needed his guidance in my life. This was the prompt I needed to finally stop running from him, and we prayed and I gave my life to God.

Jacqui's appointment to see me came in the middle of a very desperate situation. One of the doorstep lenders was demanding a payment of £110 that I simply could not make. I had just £3 in my purse. Jacqui stepped into the situation with such confidence, faith and prayer. She asked God for a miracle and sent a text message to her prayer team to pray for me. I was blown away; within half an hour, one offered to pay the entire balance and wipe the debt. The other two offered to clear the remaining balance that I owed to two other local money lenders. In less than an hour, a hopeless situation was completely transformed. The pressure was lifted in an instant and I was overwhelmed by the grace and love that was shown to me. I vowed to work with CAP with everything I had.

They put together a budget for me and sorted out all the finances into something that I could understand. By setting up a CAP Account that I paid into, they would do the rest; working behind the scenes to negotiate better settlements and handling all the paperwork. It was hard at first, but I remained disciplined, knowing it was for the best. I could see myself slowly getting out of debt and it was an incredible feeling.

It took two years of sticking to my budget to get out of debt. I gradually paid off each one and, in March 2010, there was nobody left to pay. The CAP budget is amazing. I even managed to save £100, which is something I had never been able to do before. I used some of the money to treat my little one on his birthday. Sticking to the budget really works!

There has been an undeniable change in me since my encounter with God in the sea. It's like coming out of a cloud and seeing the light at the end of the tunnel. I do have worries, but I know I can cope and get through anything with God to help me. The struggle with my eldest son has gotten easier. He finds it hard to accept the change, but I have the strength to say no. I look to the Bible for advice and have become much more responsible through it. I discipline my kids so that they will learn and grow as people. Hard decisions I have to make are still difficult, but I know that they are for the best. The way I see it, I was a good mother before, but not a godly mother. God has been my guide and helped me, and I know that my children will benefit from the change.

My ten-year-old daughter, Lisa, gave her life to Jesus in 2011 at the CAP Christmas party and my two youngest boys now follow Jesus. It is the most magical and overwhelming thing to experience as a parent. Harvey, aged seven, said to me, 'I have asked Jesus into my heart'. A few weeks later he said, 'I'll never deny Jesus.'

I got a call from my brother who I hadn't spoken to for more than two years. He called to say that he had seen me on a CAP DVD, which had been played whilst he was at church with his fiancée. 'I nearly fell off my chair when I saw my sister on the screen!' he said.

He told me that he had become a Christian just a few months earlier and that he was so proud of me. The following day our mum also gave her life to the Lord. My family has been brought together; relationships that were severed have been bound back together in God's love.

I feel like I have also inherited a new family at church. I am surrounded by people who genuinely care and want to support me. I know that if I have troubles, I can bring them to church and know that I will be prayed for. My pastor is a constant encouragement through all life can throw at me, and he has been like a father to me. My boys are surrounded by strong male figures that can show a Godly example. Church is a safe place; I walk through the doors and feel a sense of peace and the living presence of God. Times are still tough, even now I'm debt-free, but when I've felt weak and wondered whether I can really carry on, God and his church have kept me standing.

What I know for sure is that, without CAP, I couldn't have coped. God called me out of the water, but dealing with the mess would have been impossible on my own. The personal and loving support I received was such a powerful witness to the personal God that CAP serves. Having been supported by Christians and built up in a brilliant church, I feel like myself again – except a hundred times stronger and more secure.

Now, I don't live in guilt like I did in Joel's teenage years. Jesus has freed me and I live in the truth of his forgiveness. I'd be lying if I said life was a walk in the park now; being a Christian isn't easy and tough times still come. But the difference is that through my struggles, I have hope for the future. Jesus provides me with strength and support, and the knowledge of his unbounded love gives me a sense of belonging that I had never known. God certainly isn't fluffy – but he is good.

Creating ripples

John Kirkby

In many ways, my own journey of hope is reflected in so many of the stories you've just read. My story began in 1992, when I lost everything I had worked for; my businesses, house and marriage. I felt utterly alone, broken and without hope. I was left in huge debt that nearly destroyed me. From that depth of despair, God reached into my life with overwhelming love and compassion through a church full of people who cared. I gave my life to God in 1994 and from that time, God started to rebuild me from the inside out. I realised that God had a purpose for my life and a future for my family.

I could never have known all those years ago that God would use that darkness I'd experienced to bring light to others. By enabling me to climb out of the hole into which I'd fallen, God helped me do for myself what CAP was about to do for thousands of other people. At the beginning of 1996, I began to realise that although God had given me a new life and hope, there was more that he wanted to do with me. He wanted me to use my experience to help people who were still left in the pit of debt and darkness. So in June 1996, with my new wife Lizzie, I started Christians Against Poverty straight after returning from our honeymoon.

I still clearly remember visiting my second ever client, Debbie, in October 1996. I remember sitting in her lounge hearing of a family whose life was totally devastated and her struggle to feed her two sons Lloyd and Adam, aged nine and seven respectively. She had resorted to feeding them dumplings before bed as it was the cheapest way to stop them crying with hunger in the night. The amazing privilege of being able to show Debbie the way out of debt and stand in the gap between her and her creditors was life changing for her and her family and also for me. It gave me the encouragement I needed that this thing was worth it; it was worth all the sacrifice just to see one life changed.

Seventeen years on, debt is a bigger problem than ever in the UK, causing widespread misery, hunger, illness, desperation and suicide. The good news is that, through CAP and the local church, we are offering a real solution and an eternal hope that is transforming thousands of people's lives every year, just like Brian, Wendy, Sue and the others who you have read about in this book.

Seeing what God has done for me repeated thousands of times over is just amazing. For me, Sue Didi's story encapsulates what CAP and God's transforming power is all about. God meets us when we are broken and he gently and lovingly restores us to all our potential. He restores us into someone who is made in his image, with his heart of compassion for others and his values, focus and purpose. We then start helping others and pointing them back to their loving God. And so begins an upward circle of hope. When one life is touched, that person then reaches out to others who are hurting and so it carries on. For me that meant starting CAP; for Sue that meant becoming a CAP Job Club Coach. What will it mean for you?

These stories, and also my own experience of debt, continue to drive the deep urgency I have to reach many more people who need CAP's help. That's why we've pressed ahead to open more and more CAP Debt Centres in partnership with local churches. Our combination of financial expertise and the love of the church brings a truly life transforming mix. Not only can we offer a way out of debt, but also share the hope we have in the only one who can truly transform lives for an eternity.

This growing vision means we continually need more people to join us. I've always known that for CAP to work and to grow I can't do it alone. Along the way I have needed lots of people to join and support the work; people to pray, people to give, and people to sacrificially lay down their lives to change this nation one life at a time. The unsung heroes of this amazing work and thousands of lives transformed are our staff, volunteers, supporters and churches who partner with us throughout the UK. Without their dedication, sacrifice, hard work and determination to reach the poor with the gospel of hope, all our hopes and dreams would have come to nothing and this book could never have been written.

We need you to join the movement. Thousands of people just like you are helping the church reach the poor and proclaim the gospel of hope to them. As you read this book, I'm sure you felt God's compassion and heart for the poor. It must resonate with you and I want to ask you to make sure that you do something practical with those emotions. Through our last edition of Journeys of Hope and my book Nevertheless, thousands of people have not just read the stories, but have done something with the passion that the stories inspire.

As you reflect on the stories you've read, my heart is that you will be inspired to do something. Can you pray for us? Can you support us financially with just a few pounds a month and join thousands of people in our Life Changer programme? Can you get involved either directly with your local church or inspire your church to get involved in the work of CAP?

We need you, the Church needs you, the poor and needy in your neighbourhood need you, and God needs you to fulfil his heart of justice and mercy for the poor of this nation. Do it today. Chances are, if you put it off, the moment will pass, everyday life will take over and you'll forget those feelings that God has stirred in you. Fill in a Life Changer form from the back of this book, get on our website, join our prayer team or contact your pastor. Do it soon; don't let anything get in the way of you joining and supporting us to see thousands more journeys of hope unfold.

Thank you

John Kirkby
Founder & International Director

Become a
Life Changer *by making a monthly gift*
changing lives, one life at a time

---

nt to become a Life Changer / increase my regular donation

e would like to make a monthly gift of £3☐ £5☐ £10☐ £20☐ £50☐ or £ _____

1st ☐ 8th ☐ 15th ☐ 28th ☐ **(please select)** of each month until further notice.

t payment will be made in _____ (please state month)

uld like to increase my existing monthly gift from £ _____ to £ _____

---

details – please complete in BLOCK CAPITALS (by filling in this form, you are confirming you are over 16 years old)

Name:

e of address:

Postcode:

one: Mobile:

Birth: `D D M M Y Y`   Where did you get this form from? _____

Aid declaration

UK taxpayer and I would like Christians Against Poverty to reclaim tax   ☐ I am **not** a UK taxpayer

eat as Gift Aid donations all qualifying gifts of money made:
in the future ☐   today ☐   in the past 4 years ☐   in the future ☐   (please tick all that apply)

ure _____   `D D M M Y Y`

e paid or will pay an amount of Income Tax and/or Capital Gains Tax for each tax year (6 April to 5 April) that is at least equal to the amount of tax that all the charities or Community Clubs (CASCs) that I donate to will reclaim on my gifts for that tax year. I understand that other taxes such as VAT and Council Tax do not qualify. I understand the charity will reclaim every £1 that I give. Please notify Christians Against Poverty if you change your name and/or address. Reg. Charity N° 1097217.

---

uctions to your bank/Building Society to pay by Direct Debit

nager:
ding Society _____   Originators Identification N°. `8 3 7 3 8 5`   **DIRECT Debit**

ding Society address: _____

tion to your bank/Building Society

y Christians Against Poverty Direct Debits from the account detailed in this instruction, subject to the safeguards assured ect Debit Guarantee. I understand that this instruction may remain with Christians Against Poverty and if so, details will be ctronically to my bank/Building Society.

s) of account holder(s) _____

e `☐☐☐☐☐☐`   Bank/Building Society account number `☐☐☐☐☐☐☐☐`

ure _____   `D D M M Y Y`

Building Societies may not accept Direct Debit instructions for some types of account

ffice: Jubilee Mill, North Street, Bradford, BD1 4EW **e** info@capuk.org **t** 01274 760720 **w** capuk.org
harity No. 1097217 **Charity Registered in Scotland** No. SC038776 **Company Limited by Guarantee, Registered in England and Wales** No. 4655175

---

ect Debit Guarantee: The Direct Debit Guarantee should be detached and retained by the payer.   **DIRECT Debit**

ee is offered by all banks & Building Societies that accept instructions to pay Direct Debits. If there are any changes to date or frequency of your Direct Debit, Christians Against Poverty will notify you 10 working days in advance of your account being debited or as reed. If you request Christians Against Poverty to collect a payment, confirmation of the amount & date will be given to you at the time of the request. If ade in the payment of your Direct Debit, by Christians Against Poverty or your bank or Building Society, you are entitled to a full and immediate refund at paid from your bank or Building Society. If you receive a refund you are not entitled to, you must pay it back when Christians Against Poverty asks an cancel a Direct Debit at any time by simply contacting your bank or Building Society. Written confirmation may be required. Please also notify us.

I am a *Life Changer*

because...

We asked our supporters to tell us why they support CAP with a regular donation. It was amazing to hear people's heart for the poor!

CAP has over 21,000 monthly givers, called Life Changers. Join them at **capuk.org/lifechangers**.

Rosie Andrews

Knowing your money helps people come into contact with Jesus for themselves is the best thing ever!

Lizi Bowerman

You were there when I needed you most and liberated me without judgement or critism, but with God's love and mercy.

Julia Childerhous

God has asked m to be a steward o his money and to give what I have to those who hav not. CAP is a grea way of doing tha

Ruth Davies

Because God is in the business of changing lives and I like workin with him.

Benjamin Alexander

Bad debt is one of the great ills of modern society. CAP can do a lot more with my money than I can and they are doing it from the same motivation as I have.

sina Greenwell

cause CAP
abled me to
come debt
e and be in
position to
lp others.

hn Cherry

m a Life
hanger
ecause
sus was!

yrus Bhandara

was in a
ark place
nancially and
AP held mine
nd my wife's
and through
all.

Deborah Sweet

It's absolutely brilliant to hear the testimonies of people's lives being released from the grip of poverty. Everyone deserves to live free from worry and fear. CAP releases people from the prison of debt. That's why I am a Life Changer.

The average Life Changer donates £12.41 a month to CAP. **Life Changers are our main source of income.**

Leaving an
eternal legacy

CAP has already seen thousands of lives transformed from a place of despair to one of hope. We invite you to be a part of ensuring this life changing work continues in the future by choosing to leave CAP a legacy in your will.

For your free legacy pack, call 01274 761980 or visit capuk.org/legacy.

'In the future, CAP will still need funding, so I really wanted to leave money behind. For me, this is one way of working for justice.'
Carole, CAP legacy pledger